THE UTAH SCHOOL SYSTEM:

Its Organization and Administration

REUBEN D. LAW
DEAN, COLLEGE OF EDUCATION
BRIGHAM YOUNG UNIVERSITY

Provo, Utah
Brigham Young University Press
1952

INTRODUCTION AND ACKNOWLEDGEMENTS

This material has been written for the benefit of students of education in colleges and universities, teachers and administrators in the field, and interested laymen who wish to enlarge their information and understandings regarding the school system.

Extensive portions of the material have been developed and actively used in connection with the teaching of courses in educational organization and school law. The writer is indebted to hundreds of students who have frankly given their reactions and evaluations in ways that have been especially helpful. A sabbatical leave granted by President Ernest L. Wilkinson and the Board of Trustees of Brigham Young University made it possible to find the time in which to do the final writing.

Grateful acknowledgement is made to my colleagues, Dr. A. Reed Morrill, Professor Owen L. Barnett, and Dr. J. C. Moffitt for their many acts of helpfulness in relation to this work; to Dr. F. Allen Bateman, Dr. William P. Miller, and State School Office staff for advance copies of legislative enactments and various types of data; to Dr. Franklin L. West for supplying the data regarding the founding of the church academies; to officials and secretaries in the colleges and universities who responded to requests for information; to the authors of publications from which quotations are entered in this volume; to my wife, Leda, for proof reading the manuscript; and to all others who have provided help and encouragement.

4

CONTENTS

Introduction and Acknowledgements 3

List of Figures, Charts, and Tables 8

Chapter:

I SOME BASIC GUIDING PRINCIPLES 11
Principles; system of values; the good and the better, education essential to democracy; democratic
organization; individual and society; integration;
active process; controversial issues; responsive to
the people; character education; free from sectarian or partisan control; servant of educative process;
use of initiative; continuous growth and planning;
selective admission; service to the good life; state
function; size of district; free schools; compulsory
attendance; investment in progress; equalization of
educational opportunity; six essentials; platform of
A.A.S.A.; resolutions of A.A.S.A.; platform of
N.E.A.; bibliography.

II SOME BACKGROUND INFLUENCES 41
Religious influences; civic mindedness; the westward movement; consolidation; some evidences of
educational accomplishment; what of the future;
bibliography.

III DESCRIPTIVE OVERVIEW OF
EDUCATIONAL ORGANIZATION 65
Education a state function; legal basis for school
system; state board of education, superintendent,
and staff; school districts as arms of the state; forty
school districts; consolidation; district organization;
adult education; school districts in the forty-eight
states; character education and school-community
relations; balanced growing; safeguards against
sectarian or partisan control; vocational education;
state and private colleges and universities; private
schools; special schools and state agencies; bibliography.

IV THE STATE DEPARTMENT OF
    PUBLIC INSTRUCTION 80
    State board of education; number of board mem-
    bers, term of office, how selected; nomination and
    election of members of state board of education;
    chairman and vice-chairman; appointment of state
    superintendent; secretary; assistants and staff;
    compensation and expense of board members; fill-
    ing of unexpired terms; duties of state superintend-
    ent and staff; board responsible directly to the
    people; bibliography.

V THE ORGANIZATION & ADMINISTRATION
    OF THE SCHOOL DISTRICT 90
    Arm of the state; board of education; election of
    board members; qualifications of board members;
    filling of unexpired terms; organization of board;
    compensation and expenses; body corporate; com-
    mittee of the whole; joint rather than individual
    authority; president and vice-president; superin-
    tendent of schools; clerk and treasurer; audit;
    principal; teachers and pupils; liabilities; display
    of flag; transportation of pupils; safety patrols;
    course of study and textbooks; libraries; other items
    related to the school district; bibliography.

VI THE ORGANIZATION AND MANAGEMENT
    OF THE INDIVIDUAL SCHOOL 112
    Function of administration; principal; types of
    organization; administrative relationships; a test
    for the teacher; extension of home life; school
    management; teacher-pupil relations; nature of
    standards; understanding the individual child; sec-
    ondary schools; elementary schools; grouping;
    secret societies; reporting to parents; records and
    reports; bibliography.

VII FINANCING ELEMENTARY AND
    SECONDARY EDUCATION IN UTAH 129
    High efficiency with moderate expenditures per
    pupil; greater effort; per cent of income spent for

education; biased propaganda; constitutional amendments; early territorial and state aid; minimum school program; local leeway; minimum educational requirements; school budgets; audit; funds for sites, buildings, and equipment; building reserve fund; special tax; bonded indebtedness; approval of plans and specifications; need for broadening tax base; conclusion; bibliography.

VIII COLLEGES AND UNIVERSITIES 146

Early attention to higher education; ten colleges and universities; financial support; governing bodies; enrollment; instruction in the U. S. constitution; no partisan or denominational doctrine as qualification; out-of-state fees; teacher education and certification; variety of study fields; history and present status; state institutions; private institutions; bibliography.

IX TEACHER RETIREMENT 152

Founding of retirement system; retirement board; retirement fund; contributions by members; retirement of non-teacher employees; membership required; eligibility for retirement; retirement allowance; disability retirement; withdrawal before retirement; reentering after withdrawal; benefits to beneficiary in case of death; local city systems; retirement systems of private institutions; retirement as earned income; professionally and sociologically desirable; bibliography.

X THE FEDERAL GOVERNMENT AND
    EDUCATION 162

U. S. Constitution; U. S. Office of Education; Recommendation of A.A.S.A.; appropriations for education; vocational education; research; veterans' education; military education; National Science Foundation; medical education; extension services; aid to war congested communities; education for children of U. S. officials and employees in foreign countries; education in the territories, canal zone, occupied islands, and isolated projects; international educational relations; Library of Congress; education of American Indians; vocational rehabilitation; education of the blind; loans for housing of faculty members and students; war surplus commodities and equipment; school lunch; land grants and proceeds from lands; the issue of federal aid to education; bibliography.

XI HOME - SCHOOL - COMMUNITY
  RELATIONS 180

Reciprocal relationships; community school; importance of public relations; the pupil and public relations; professional teachers; reports to parents; the P.T.A.; National Citizens Commission for the Public Schools; National Commission for the Defense of Democracy; N.E.A. Division of Press and Radio Relations; avenues to the public; television and the F.C.C.; films; community coordinating councils; compulsory attendance laws; corporal punishment; health of teachers and children; handicapped children; adult education; Americanization schools; school lunch; school policies and the public; bibliography.

XII PROFESSIONALISM IN EDUCATION AND
  THE ORGANIZED PROFESSION 205

Meaning of professionalism; selective admission; objective, scientific information; service motive; membership in professional organizations; code of professional ethics; conclusion; bibliography.

APPENDIX 222

Scriptural references to education
Miscellaneous references

LIST OF FIGURES, CHARTS, AND TABLES

Figure I.　Utah School Districts 9

Charts:

I.　Line and Staff Relationships in the
　　School District 105

II.　Plan of Organization of the U. S.
　　Office of Education 163

Tables:

I.　Academies Established by the Church of
　　Jesus Christ of Latter-day Saints 47

II.　Per cent of Those 6-13 Enrolled in
　　Elementary Schools 60

III.　Per cent of Those 14-17 Enrolled in
　　Secondary Schools 61

IV.　Per cent of Those 18-21 Enrolled in
　　Colleges and Universities 61

V.　Number of School Districts in the
　　Forty-Eight States 72

VI.　Expelled from School for Inability to Learn 120

VII.　Members' Rates of Contributions to
　　Retirement System in Percentage of Salary 154

Figure I

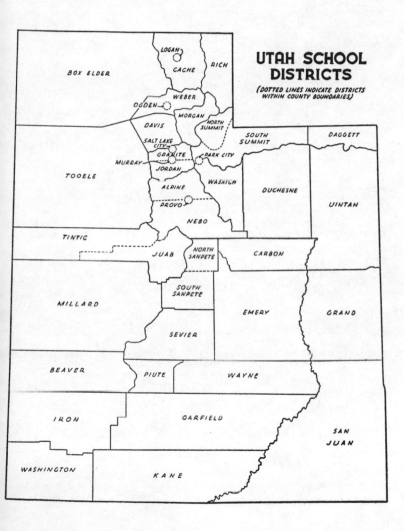

Figure 1

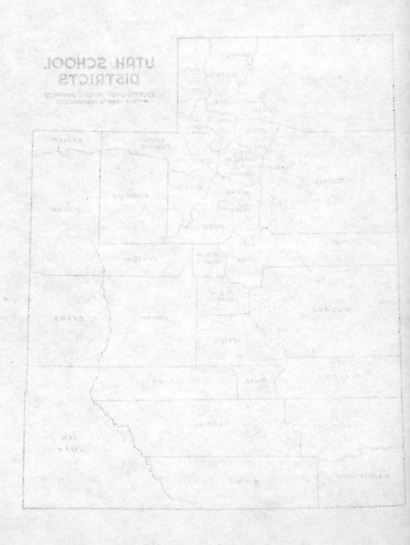

CHAPTER I

SOME BASIC, GUIDING PRINCIPLES

Princi-
ples
Any one embarking upon a study of the organization and operation of schools, or any one intending to participate in the work of the schools, either as a professional worker or as a lay supporter, should actively be mindful of certain basic principles which are vital to our democratic society in providing for the education of its citizenry.

It is recognized that entire books have been devoted to principles of education and philosophy of education, and a whole set of books would be needed to do justice to this area. However, for our purposes in relation to the present study, a limited number of principles and criteria are selected to be called to the reader's attention in the hope that he will think deeply about them, discuss them with others, and apply them in his work. They are here given only brief treatment, and no attempt is made to arrange them in order of importance. By their very nature they cannot be kept mutually exclusive, but are closely interrelated.

System
of
Values
One's philosophy is one's system of values. As you have been struggling for orientation in the many phases of life you have been reaching out for a system of values by which to determine which things are of most worth in life. This is a never ending quest, and, as you make progress in understanding and in the pursuit of worthy purposes, your system of values or your philosophy of life and education should become a truer and more adequate one. For education and life are inseparably connected and should not be regarded separately. A great philosopher defined education as "life, growth, social process, and the continuous

reconstruction of experience"[1]. It has too often been regarded only as preparation *for* life instead of being associated *with* life. Are you growing in your interpretation
of life's values, and what difference is it making in what
you choose to do? If you have decided to become a teacher
what are the things in relation to your system of values
which influenced that decision? Have you discussed this
decision with your teachers or counselors? If you are a
lay supporter what are the values which prompt that
support?

*The Good
and the
Better*

It should be noted that in applying our
system of values the choice is not always between the good and the bad. The choice is
often between the good and the better. Probably the greatest enemy of the best in education is the
moderately good in education with which we become com-
placently satisfied.

*Essential
to
Democracy*

Education is essential to democracy.
"From our colonial beginnings to the present statesmen have asserted, and citizens
have affirmed, the claim of education to a
unique position in our republican form of government.
Leaders in government and in education today more than
ever are aware that freedom of choice for the individual
can be reconciled with the common good only through the
proper education of all citizens. They recognize further
that assaults upon our free institutions and the liberties of
individuals can be withstood only by a citizenry thoroughly educated in the democratic processes and fortified by
the ability to use knowledge and resources to attain good
ends. Citizens share with statesmen a growing consciousness that our ability to maintain and extend our democratic institutions is determined both by the kind of education provided and by the ways in which it is provided".[2]

1. John Dewey.
2. Council of State Governments: The Forty-eight State School Systems.
Chicago, Illinois, 1949, p. 4.

Democratic Organization   To serve democracy education must be democratic in its organization and procedure. In a very real sense the *way* we teach and the *way* we operate our schools become an important part of *what* we teach, or in other words, that which is learned by the pupils. People learn what they live in relation to time, place, persons, and conditions. Racial discriminations, as well as discriminations on the basis of religion or partisan politics, should find no place in the operation of public schools in a democracy.

Individual and Society   Education must be adapted to and serve the current and long range needs of both society and the individual, with effective attention to the interests and maturation level of the pupils, individually and as a group. Man is an end in himself and not a mere means to an end.[3] The human personality is sacredly important, and the value and function of education in the building of that personality should not be regarded lightly. The best school is not necessarily the most difficult one, certainly not the most arbitrary in its program. The best school is the one in which the pupils do the most desirable balanced growing in relation to needs and stage of development and through which the democratic society and the individuals in that society are best served.

Integration   Integration is balanced growing, physically, intellectually, socially, spiritually, and emotionally. It is fostered by a wholesome and sensibly balanced variety of experiences providing for perceptual, sensori-motor, memory, problem solving, and affective learnings under conditions conducive to growth.

Active Process   Learning is an active process which can be done only by the learner. Teaching involves selecting, planning, stimulating, guiding, directing, and evaluating activities which facilitate learning

---

3. This is a basic difference between democracy and totalitarianism.

in a setting planned to enhance desirable learning. Good teaching recognizes the need for satisfying experiences in purposing, planning, executing, and evaluating on the part of the pupils. The strength of a democracy rests on the ability and inclination of people continually to make wise choices. One best learns to make wise choices through satisfying experiences in successfully making wise choices. Similar conclusions may be drawn about such other important lessons for democratic living as learning to abide by the decisions of the majority, learning to take and to give constructice criticism, learning to cooperate for the common good, and to differ with others courteously, with obvious implications for the school in its procedures.

Controversial   Although the schools must be thor-
Issues   oughly fair and discrete and highly ob-
              jective in their approach to controversial
issues, they should not be deprived of considering objectively the pros and cons of any and all controversial issues. If the schools were left with only those materials related to things which all groups and individuals would regard as entirely noncontroversial, they would be left with only the husks under a gag rule which would itself jeopardize the safety of democracy.

Responsive   School systems should be so organized as
to the   to be responsive to the will of the people as
People   a whole, and, at the same time be protected
              from the upsetting derogatory attempts of
temporary, disturbing minorities and selfish interest groups.

Character   The schools cannot be neutral in matters
Education   of character education as affecting the indi-
              vidual and society.[4] The right kind of education should be a means of social and individual betterment.

---

4. See Educational Policies Commission, N.E.A.: Moral and Spiritual Values in the Public Schools. 1201 Sixteenth Street, N.W., Washington, D. C. 1951.

Free from
Sectarian
or Partisan
Control
Public education must be free from sectarian control and free from partisan political control. Boards of education, state and district, should be responsible directly to the people and not to political bodies or political officials. Accordingly, boards of education should be elected by the people in a non-partisan election at a time other than the regular political election. School employees are responsible through executives to boards of education and through them to the people. Such system and order should be a protection to society and to the teachers who must be free to fearlessly pursue the truth wherever it leads.

Servant of
Educative
Process
Educational organization and administration must be the servant of the educative process in providing services and conditions which facilitate teaching and learning. To enhance the rendering of such service organizational and administrative relationships and divisions of responsibility should be clearly defined. When persons are charged with responsibilities they should be vested with the necessary authority to fulfill those responsibilities, subject, of course, to the will of the majority of those concerned. However, it should be recognized that the authority of expertness and real service is preferable for frequent use to the authority of position.

Use of
Initiative
Good administration encourages rather than discourages effective use of initiative by the staff, and operates under a policy of responsible leadership through highly democratic procedures in which all who are influenced by important decisions may have opportunity to influence the making of those decisions. In a democracy teachers should expect to serve on curriculum committees and other committees in a cooperative effort to improve the effectiveness of the school. Likewise, community schools seek the cooperation of its

patrons and the various constructive groups and organizations in the community.

Continuous Growth and Planning   Good teaching involves continuous growth on the part of the teacher as well as on the part of those whom he teaches. Education involves continuous, constructive planning, not haphazard performance. Modern education with its greater adjustment to the needs and interests of pupils, though more flexible, involves more and better planning than was formerly required.

Selective Admission   Teaching in the public schools is not a right to be demanded by any citizen. It is a privilege to be granted by society on the basis of ability and worthiness.[5]

Service to the Good Life   Persons entering the teaching profession must recognize the opportunity for rendering satisfying, unselfish service, and also the inherent obligation to direct one's own personal living in line with the ethical and moral standards of the better elements of the community.[6] "The teacher takes his whole self to teaching."[7] "The best of good teaching comes as an overflow of satisfying life."[8]

Loyalties   Teaching involves loyalties of the highest order, loyalties to great principles, to the democratic society of which we are members, to the educative process by which that society is maintained and improved, loyalties to pupils, to fellow workers, and loyalties to the organized profession.[9]

State Function   The organization and control of education is essentially a state function. The school district is an arm of the state and draws its authority from the people of the entire state through consti-

---

5. Law, Reuben D.: Content and Criteria Relating to Professional Teacher Education. University of Southern California, Los Angeles, 1941.

6. See U.E.A. Code of Ethics.

7. A. S. Barr, University of Wisconsin.

8. Entorf.

9. The organized profession as such is discussed in Chapter XII.

tutional and statutory law. State responsibility for education is firmly entrenched in the constitutions of the various states along with a generally accepted conviction that a considerable share of local control is both desirable and essential through statutory provision for the same by state legislatures.

Size of District   School districts should be of sufficient size to provide optimum possibilities for efficiency and professionalism in the operation of schools, and for attracting and holding competent, well prepared teachers and administrators.

Free Schools   Democratic education must be free to all the children of all the people, rich and poor, through elementary and secondary schools up to an acceptable state minimum. The President's Committee on Education recommended free education to and including the fourteenth grade. In line with this important principle of universal education, the constitutional law and the statute law of this state, as in most other states, prohibits the charging of tuition for admission to public elementary or secondary schools.[10] Although small student body activity fees are generally permitted in secondary schools, the charging of special fees for so-called special phases of the school program is regarded as a violation of the long established principle of free public education.

Compulsory Attendance   School attendance is not only a democratic privilege, but also a duty in the interest of the individual and society. Compulsory attendance laws are provided as a protection against exploitation of children and youth and as a safeguard to society.

---

10. School Laws of the State of Utah, Article X, Sections 1 and 2, p. 7, and 75-9-7, p. 43. 1951.

Investment
In Progress
Money spent for good education is an investment in the progress of people, an investment which pays remarkable dividends.[11] In the long run, the neglect of education is costly in many ways both to the individual and to society.

Equalization of
Educational
Opportunity
A very important principle in the financing of schools is the equalization principle brought i n t o operation through broadening the tax base over a larger area. The number of children and youth to be educated and the amount of taxable wealth for the support of education are very unevenly distributed geographically, making it essential to tax the wealth where it is to educate the children where they are. The obligation of the entire state in support of this principle is recognized by constitutional and statute law. Without the operation of this principle the schools in some localities would be impoverished and the education of the children seriously limited, to their detriment as well as the detriment of society generally.

Opponents in the form of selfish interest groups have at times tried to gain advantage by name calling, branding this practice of equalization as socialism, but it is really far from objectionable socialism in the popular connotation of the term.[12] Instead, it is a long standing, fundamental American principle of equalization of educational opportunity for the masses. "The principle of taxing wealthy areas of a city or state to support education in less wealthy areas was settled in the United States. . . . more than a century ago. It was confirmed as constitutional by the Supreme Court."[13]

---

11. U. S. Chamber of Commerce, Committee on Education: Education, an Investment in People. U. S. Chamber of Commerce Bldg., Washington, D. C. 1944.

12. If this is socialism then all taxation, local, state, and national ,in which each man does not personally get returns in services in exact proportion to the size of his tax, is socialism.

13. Dr. E. Allen Bateman. Provo Herald, April 22, 1951.

Six
Essentials

The following six essentials for the "sound administration and operation of our state school systems" are stated in a publication by the Council of State Governments:[14]

"1. Provision for systematically obtaining and studying the facts as a basis for policy decisions;

2. A state policy-making agency for education through which the will of the people may be voiced and the interests of the state protected;

3. Local administrative units of sufficient size to promote effective local control and to provide appropriate educational opportunities at a reasonable cost;

4. Provisions calculated to assure high quality professional leadership for both state and local agencies;

5. Conditions conducive to maintaining well-qualified staffs of teachers for all phases of elementary and secondary education;

6. A system of financing that will provide sufficient funds and distribute them in such a way as to assure adequate educational opportunities for all and to encourage both sound administration and a high degree of local initiative."[14]

Platform
of A.A.S.A.

Because of its significance in relation to foundation principles there is quoted below the Platform of the American Association of School Administrators:[15]

14. Council of State Governments: The Forty-Eight State School Systems, Chicago, Ill. 1949, pp. 7 & 8.
15. Adopted at national convention, Atlantic City, N. J., March 5, 1947.

PLATFORM

Preamble: As Americans we cherish our heritage of freedom as expressed in the Bill of Rights. We regard our freedom as a sacred trust which imposes upon each of us an obligation to help build a society in which respect for the individual is recognized as the basis of all human rights. In such a society opportunity is provided for the political, social, economic, educational, and spiritual welfare of all its citizens. In the belief that public education provides the only certain means for the achievement of these ends by the individual and by the nation, we—the members of the American Association of School Administrators—pledge ourselves to the support of the program and principles contained in this platform.

A. As American citizens we believe—

1. That peace in this age is a requisite to all other qualities of individual and group welfare.

2. That democrary is a fundamental promise for the solution of all social, economic, and political problems.

3. That education is the greatest constructive force at the disposal of democratic peoples for the solution of their problems.

4. That every privilege in a democracy must be matched by an equal responsibility.

5. That the strength of the nation will depend upon the conservation and intelligent development of our human and natural resources.

6. That progress in our social, economic, and political life must keep pace with changes in our material and technological environment; such progress can result only from a better program of education and spiritual growth.

B.   As educators we believe—

1. That universal free education must be made available by all peoples in the interests of world understanding, citizenship, and peace.

2. That the perpetuation of American democracy requires universal free education fitted to the abilities, interests, and needs of each person.

3. That social, civic, economic, spiritual, and vocational competencies are as important as academic literacy.

4. That the purpose of American education is full participation in democratic living by all members of society.

5. That the school program should emphasize the worth and dignity of all essential work.

6. That the quality of education will be determined by the quality of the persons who teach.

7. That the structure of American school systems should be adaptable enough to meet the educational needs of all age levels in a changing society.

8. That the total educational experience of each individual must be designed to contribute to the development of effective ethical character.

C.   Inorder that these principles may be realized in American life, we as school administrators propose to work for—

1. Professionally competent administrative leadership, dedicated to the service of good teaching in every community.

2. The recruitment, preparation, and in-service growth of outstanding individuals as teachers, administrators, and other professional workers to assure good teaching.

3. Salaries and conditions which will attract and retain good teachers.

4. Smaller classes, more individualized teaching, and more adequate materials and equipment—thus providing a better educational program for each child.

5. Wide sharing with teachers and others in the cooperative formulation of educational policies and programs on local, state, and national levels.

6. School districts large enough to meet modern educational needs effectively and economically.

7. A program of lay participation in education which will lead to an intelligent appreciation of the work and needs of the schools.

8. Federal support of education, in an average amount of at least fifty cents per day for each child enrolled in publicly supported and controlled schools, administered through the U. S. Office of Education and state departments of education.

9. Complete fiscal independence of local boards of education.

10. An extended use of all school facilities.[16]

Resolutions of A.A.S.A. Students of education will also be interested in the resolutions adopted by the American Association of School Administrators, February 21, 1951, at Atlantic City, New Jersey,[17] and also the Platform of the National Education Association.[18]

---

16. Formulated by the Planning Committee and adopted by vote of the members in attendance at the A.A.S.A. Atlantic City convention, March 5, 1947.

17. The American Association of School Administrators is a department of the National Education Association.

18. Report of Committee on Resolutions to the Representative Assembly of the National Education Association of the United States, Cleveland, Ohio, July 9, 1948.

RESOLUTIONS
AMERICAN ASSOCIATION OF
SCHOOL ADMINISTRATORS

1. *American public schools and the strength of the nation.* The American Association of School Administrators believes that the American system of free public schools is the indispensible foundation for the development and survival of our form of democracy. The forces of freedom may be at present outnumbered. Strength in any aspect of manpower, however, is a product of quality as well as of quantity. Free public education has given us our margin of safety. It is the basis of our unparalleled technology and productivity and of our determination to perpetuate our free way of life.

Hence, in the present emergency situation, which promises to be long continued, our free public education is as important to our defense as guns, ships, or planes.

Our government—local, state, and federal—in its efforts to strengthen the defense of the nation cannot afford to neglect or to subordinate our schools either with regard to the education of youth or to the provision of necessary materials for that education.

2. *Military service.* We reaffirm our support of an adequate national defense plan in which all the resources of the nation are utilized, including the cooperative development and use of school facilities.

We believe, without reservation, that the needs of national security must be adequately met at all times through provision of the necessary strength for the armed forces and maintenance of a continuing flow of trained personnel into the civil economy. We believe that the existing emergency can be met best by a revised and strengthened system of Selective Service which will reevaluate the standards of eligibility for admission into the armed services. As far as possible, persons should be accepted for limited service if they fail to qualify for combat.

Such factors as the timing of induction and choice and duration of service should be so arranged that the educational careers of youth at the secondary level need not be interrupted and opportunities for higher education under civilian auspices shall not be eliminated.

We oppose any form of legislation which, in the name of national security, sets up parallel educational agencies that absorb, supplant, or duplicate the educational facilities now in existence.

3. *Critical materials for education.* The grave responsibility of education, coupled with the upward surge in school population and the great lag in schoolhouse construction, constitutes an important phase of the national emergency which must be met by immediate federal action providing adequately for an assured flow of critical materials for essential schoolhouse construction, equipment, and supplies.

When the system of priorities and allocations is established, the needs of the schools must be considered as an integral part of the national defense effort.

4. *Inflation.* Since inflation is as serious a menace to education as it is to other phases of defense, we urge the federal government to eliminate factors which would continue the inflationary trend.

5. *United Nations.* We urge continued use of the United Nations as an instrument of peace. We declare ourselves in favor of charter amendments to enable the United Nations to enact, interpret, and enforce world law to prevent war.

Since the United Nations is the tangible, organized expression of mankind's desire for peace ,all schools should cooperate in supporting the United Nations Education Service to be inaugurated by the National Education Association in September 1951.

6. *UNESCO.* The inclusion of references to education in the United Nations Charter, and the subsequent

establishment of the United Nations Educational, Scientific and Cultural Organization (UNESCO) are major achievements in which the teaching profession of the United States may proudly claim a substantial share. We call upon all school systems to familiarize themselves with the UNESCO program and to do their utmost to give effect to it.

We again urge the Secretary of State, in view of the critical role of our . public schools in advancing the UNESCO program, to include in future delegations to UNESCO General Conferences a substantial representation of the administrators and teachers in the public elementary and secondary schools.

7. *Occupied areas.* We reaffirm our belief that in the occupied areas of Europe and Japan, the program of education and re-education should be given a high priority. We commend the progress made in Japan which is signalized by the establishment of decentralized school systems operated by local boards of education, and urge that responsible United States officials continue their friendly and constructive interest in these programs. We strongly urge that appropriations for this purpose be commensurate with the fundamental importance of the task. Educational institutions in the United States should grant leaves of absence wherever possible to personnel invited to serve in the occupied areas.

We further recommend the immediate appointment of a new commission of outstanding American educators, including experienced administrators, whose job it will be to survey the educational needs and conditions in Germany. This commission should also offer a plan that is designed to meet these needs, giving careful attention to self-help on the part of the German people and the development of an educational program that is consistent with democratic principles.

8. *Professional status of the superintendency.* The impact of world crisis on our American way of life em-

phasizes the need for intelligent and competent educational leadership in school administration. We recognize the necessity of continuous study of the role of the school administrator as an educational leader, and pledge our support in behalf of developing plans and procedures for the improvement of the professional status of the superintendent of schools at local community, district, city, county, and state levels. The Association reaffirms its belief that further professionalization of the school administrator is desirable and essential to the welfare of children, youth, and adults.

9. *Conservation of natural and human resources.* In order to develop and conserve our human and natural resources, it is recommended that renewed emphasis be given in school curricula to the wise use of natural resources, the development of the fundamental principles of moral character and responsible citizenship, and the preparation needed for living in the world of today.

10. *Moral and spiritual values.* Because the survival and well-being of our country depend upon moral standards and spiritual values, we welcome the timely appearance of "Moral and Spiritual Values in the Public Schools," a report by the Educational Policies Commission of this Association and of the National Education Association. We urge that the members of our Association read this volume, distribute it widely throughout the profession, and make it known to the public.

11. *Teaching personnel.* Recruiting and educating competent teachers is fundamental to the improvement of the public schools.

We urge the adoption of a minimum standard of four years of college preparation, including professional courses, for the certification of teachers in all public schools. We further recommend that adequate inservice training programs be provided in order that teachers may receive the most effective guidance and direction as they grow in service.

We urge that prospective teachers be carefully screened and given more guidance and counseling concerning the qualifications and requirements for successful teaching.

We must continue to strive for improved working conditions and professional recognition for teachers in order that they may be of better service in meeting the problems of our times.

We charge the teaching profession with the obligation of providing the best defense of democracy through full participation in making democracy live and work. Members of the Communist Party shall not be employed in our schools.

We urge that all agencies dealing with manpower problems give careful consideration to the development of a manpower policy which would insure the continued strength of our educational system.

We believe in strong professional organizations of teachers, local, state, and national, to improve the status of teaching and teachers.

12. *Extending educational opportunity.* We recommend the universal establishment of free public schools for all children and youth from the kindergarten through Grade XIV, and appropriate educational opportunities for adults. We deem it most urgent that the American public be specifically informed as to the serious implications of the increasing enrollments in the public schools.

13. *Public funds for public schools.* We believe the American tradition of separation of church and state should be vigorously and zealously safeguarded. We respect the rights of groups, including religious denominations, to maintain their own schools so long as such schools meet the educational, health, and safety standards defined by the states in which they are located. We believe that these schools should be financed entirely by their supporters. We therefore oppose all efforts to devote public funds to support these schools either directly or indirectly.

14. *Federal aid for public education without federal control.* We affirm our pledge to a program of public education which offers adequate opportunities for all. The realization of such a program is the shared responsibility of the federal government, the state, and the local community. We recommend the immediate passage of general federal aid legislation, and reiterate our position that federal aid must not jeopardize state and local control of education and that it must be channeled through the regularly constituted public school agencies.

15. *Federal aid for public school building construction.* There is a national urgency for rehabilitation and new construction of school buildings. Rising enrollments and high costs of construction make it impossible for many local districts to provide necessary buildings. We therefore recommend federal aid to local districts for capital outlay in school building construction. Special consideration should be given to districts that are congested because of federal government activities. We further recommend that such federal funds shall be channeled for distribution through the United States Office of Education and the state departments of education.

16. *United States Office of Education.* We reaffirm the position of the Association in urging Congress to establish the United States Office of Education as a non-partisan, independent agency, governed by a national board of education. This board should be composed of representative laymen, appointed by the President with the consent of the Senate for long, overlapping terms. Such board should have authority to appoint the commissioner of education, who would serve as its executive officer.

All activities affecting education at the national level now included within the jurisdiction of the Office of Education, or any which may hereafter be established or authorized by the Congress, should be under the direction of the Office; and any attempt to weaken or lessen the effectiveness of the Office by the transfer of such activities to other departments, agencies, or bureaus shall be strongly opposed by this Association.

We pledge a continuation of our cooperation and support to the United States Commissioner of Education, Earl James McGrath, and the United States Office of Education.

17. *State departments of education.* We believe that the leadership coming from state departments of education has great potentialities in determining the character and quality of public education. We recommend that state boards of education composed of lay citizens be established in all the states, and that chief state school officers be appointed by the state boards. To insure a minimum foundation program of education for all the children, adequate state financial support for schools is recommended.

18. *Reorganization and administration of school units.* We strongly recommend that citizens of every state where improvement of administrative units is needed give serious consideration to the reorganization of local school districts into administrative areas of sufficient size and resources to provide adequate educational opportunities for all, to attract and hold competent educational leadership, to make efficient use of educational resources, maintain effective local control, and to secure participation of lay citizens in planning the broad aspects of the educational program.

19. *Cooperative planning by school and community groups.* We reaffirm our faith in cooperative planning by school and community groups in order to serve better the needs of youth and society. All such cooperative activities must be carried on in close relationship with the board of education, the body legally constituted to operate the schools.

20. *Accreditation of teacher education institutions.* We recognize that society's increasing demands upon the public schools of America make necessary higher stand-

ards of teacher preparation and higher standards for the preparation of administrators. We heartily commend the activities of the N.E.A. National Commission on Teacher Education and Professional Standards, and the AASA Cooperative Program in Educational Administration. We similarly commend the American Association of Colleges for Teacher Education for the development of a sound pioneering of accreditation of institutions engaged in the education of teachers. We recommend that our association take steps in cooperation with other professional education associations to study the accreditation of institutions of higher learning which engage in the preparation of teachers and administrators, with a view to the development, accceptance, and general application of such national program of accreditation as later may be developed by the teaching profession.

21. *Motion pictures and television.* We believe that the offerings of the motion picture and television industries have great influence on the lives of American people; that there are in these offerings great educational opportunities; and that from them American youth, as well as people in other countries, gain many impressions as to what constitutes American life. Present offerings of these industries too often do not accurately depict our way of living. We therefore feel that education should exert its influence to the end that these industries will exercise greater care toward improving the cultural and educational quality of the motion pictures and television shows offered for American and foreign consumption. Such offerings should reflect, in so far as is practicable, the true ideals of American life. We further believe that the schools of America should correlate their efforts with these industries.

Recognizing the potentialities of television as a medium of education, we urge the Federal Communications Commission to set aside for the use of noncommercial educational television stations at least 25 per cent of the television area of the broadcasting spectrum which has not already been allocated.

22. *Expression of appreciation.* We wish to express our appreciation to the many organizations and individuals throughout America that have supported the cause of education. We are grateful for their efforts to secure greater financial assistance for our schools. Also, we appreciate their efforts to study, understand, and interpret the school program.

PLATFORM OF THE
NATIONAL EDUCATION ASSOCIATION

Platform of N.E.A. The National Education Association believes that education is the inalienable right of every American; that it is essential to our society for the promotion and preservation of democratic ideals. Therefore, the Association declares its convictions and challenges its members to leadership in attaining the objectives of this covenant.

I. *The Child*

Every child, regardless of race, belief, economic status, residence, or physical handicap, should have the opportunity for fullest development in mental, moral, social, and physical health, and in the attitudes, knowledges, habits, and skills that are essential for individual happiness and effective citizenship in a democratic nation and cooperative world. As a means to this end, the Association advocates:

A. Enriched curricula that prepare the child for his cultural, vocational, recreational, social, and civic responsibilities in a democratic nation and cooperative world, and that take into account the interests, needs, and ability of individuals.

B. Socially desirable environments that will give a

background of more fertile experience. The radio and motion pictures are of such momentous force in the life of the child that every effort should be exerted toward the continuous improvement of pictures and radio programs.

C. Expansion of our physical fitness program which will help the child to understand the scientific basis of health, physical and mental, and to develop health habits. This will include instruction regarding the effects of alcohol and narcotics upon the human body and upon society.

D. Health services that will strengthen the effectiveness of individuals as citizens. The school should fight the evils of malnutrition, nervous tension, physical ailments, and lack of physical comforts by securing adequate food, clothing, and medical care through coordinated efforts of local, state, and federal agencies for children who are in need.

E. Amendment of the Constitution of the United States to provide for the prohibition of child labor.

F. The improvement and strict enforcement of school attendance laws.

G. The right to unfettered teaching, which will aid the child to adjust himself to his environment and to changing social conditions through the development of habits of sound thinking. The fundamental principles of American democracy and world cooperation demand that students be informed concerning controversial issues.

H. Systematic programs of vocational and educational guidance, vocational placement, and follow-up, in charge of competent persons especially equipped for the work.

I. Unified community recreational programs that lead toward physical and mental health, effective citizenship, and constructive use of leisure time.

II. *The Teacher*

Teachers, regardless of position or title, are professional workers in a common cause, and, as such, have certain responsibilities and rights. The interests of the child and of the profession require:

A. Teachers of sound character and good health, with high civic ideals, who have been effectively prepared for the service which they are to perform. Their preparation should provide rich cultural background, adequate professional training, thorough knowledge of subject matter, and a well developed social consciousness.

B. Teachers who have a professional attitude in regard to self-improvement.

1. Those in service should be students of professional problems, seeking in every way to develop better educational practices.

2. Teachers should observe the principles of conduct set forth in the Code of Ethics of the National Education Association.

3. Teachers should have membership in local, state, and national education associations.

C. Teachers who are protected in their constitutional rights of freedom of speech, press, and assembly. Intellectual freedom is a public safeguard. It is the surest guarantee of orderly change and progress.

1. The teacher's conduct should be subject only to such controls as those to which other responsible citizens are subjected.

2. Teachers should have the privilege of presenting all points of view without danger of reprisal by school administrations or by pressure groups in the community.

3. Teachers should have the right of protection from intimidation through fear of loss of position,

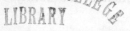

reduction of salary, loss of opportunities for advancement, or deprivation of their usual assignments, responsibilities, and authorities.

4. Teachers should have the right to organize and to support organizations that they consider to be in their own and in the public interest. Likewise, they should have the right to participate in determining school policies and school management.

D. Teachers who are protected by salaries adequate to attract and hold in the service men and women of marked ability and thorough training.

E. Teachers who are protected, in case of disability or old age, by means of sound retirement systems and, in case of financial emergency, by credit unions.

F. Teachers who are protected from discharge for political, religious, personal, or other unjust reasons by effective tenure laws.

III. *The Adult*

The adult furnishes to society leadership and vision; therefore, it is essential that he be trained in the fundamentals of education, be made responsive to the demands upon him as a citizen, and be enabled to give guidance to youth. The association advocates concerted local, state, and national efforts to attain these ends through:

A. Adult education that enriches the cultural aspects of life, prepares for parenthood, provides opportunity to develop personal talents, and emphasizes the responsibilities of democratic citizenship.

1. The existence of widespread illiteracy in the United States presents a grave problem and an insistent challenge to both laymen and teachers.

2. The minimum requirements for naturalization should include the ability to read and to write

the English language understandingly; a general knowledge of local, state, and national government; the desire to exercise the right of suffrage; and evidence of mental and economic competency. Provisions should be made to receive all persons into citizenship with suitable ceremony.

B. Unified recreational programs that will promote physical and mental health while training in the use of leisure time activities.

IV. *Organization*

A combination of national, state, and local support of public schools is necessary to provide adequate educational opportunities in all sections of the various states. For maximum effectiveness the Association believes that:

A. The federal government should study, stimulate, and support education in the interest of a high type of citizenship and should disseminate information on problems of education.

B. The state government should organize and direct education within the state.

1. The state department of education in each state should:

a. Through experimentation and leadership, stimulate local communities to provide adequate programs of education.

b. Provide and administer a system of certification of teachers based upon professional standards. The Association recommends a minimum of four years of college preparation.

c. Certify as to the adequacy of local programs of education in meeting state standards.

2. Each state should provide for a system of free schools, beginning with the nursery school and extending through the university, a full year of

not less than one hundred and eighty days in school, and class enrollment not to exceed thirty, with special attention to groups of exceptional children, and with provision for adult education.

   a. Schools for children in rural communities should be recognized as essential and integral parts of the public school system.

   b. Exceptional children, whether gifted or handicapped, should receive instruction, guidance and special care in accordance with their respective needs.

   c. Every state should provide a complete program of vocational education for youths and adults.

     (1) Classes should be organized and maintained as integral parts of local school systems.

     (2) Part-time and evening classes should be provided when necessary.

3. Every state should provide for the training of teachers and should establish standards of qualification.

C. The local district should organize and administer its school system in conformity with the standards set by the state.

1. Local district and state boards of control should be chosen on a non-partisan basis, selected at large from the areas that the board is to serve. Terms of office should be such that majority of the board will not come into office at any one time.

2. The local unit of school control should be large enough to justify the employment of men and women with special training in educational leadership for administration and supervision.

3. Lay boards should be guided by the recommendations of professional educators.
4. School budgets should be prepared by the school superintendent and his staff and adopted by the board of education.
5. The selection, promotion, and payment of teachers should be on a professional basis.
   a. Teachers of equivalent training and experience should receive equal pay regardless of sex or grade taught.
   b. Teachers should not be discriminated against because of race, color, belief, residence, or economic or marital status.

V. *Finance*

A complete program of adequate educational opportunities in all sections of the various states is essential to abundant living, to national security, and to the survival of world citizenship. To achieve this program through combined liberal support from national, state, and local sources the Association advocates:

A. A coordination of the taxing policies of national, state, and local units of government.
B. The federal government should give financial assistance to the states and territories for the support of education.
   1. Federal funds should be provided with the understanding that the expenditure of such funds and the shaping of educational policies shall be matters of state and local control.
   2. Special federal funds should be made available without federal dictation to prevent the interruption of education in devastated areas when widespread disasters occur.
   3. (Until the Congress establishes a department of

education) funds appropriated to the Office of Education should be augmented to make its efforts increasingly effective.

C. Each state should provide for the support of a complete system of free schools from public funds. The tax base should be broadened to include other sources of revenue besides real and personal property.

D. Each unit of government should be free from measures designed to place a constitutional limit on taxation within the various states.

E. Boards of education should have financial autonomy in order to fulfill their responsibilities.

F. Research workers in public finance should discover and disseminate facts concerning the best sources of revenue and their efficient expenditure.

G. A continuing program of enlightenment of the public, pupils, and teachers regarding the financial needs of the schools.

VI. *Public Relations*

Education should prepare each generation to meet the social, economic, and political problems of an ever changing world. All activities of the school should contribute to the habits and attitudes that manifest themselves in private and public life, law observance, and intelligent participation in civic affairs and world citizenship. To establish through education a closer relationship among people, the Association advocates:

A. Continuous programs to interpret to the community the aims, practices, and achievements of the schools.

B. National movements among parents and teachers to safeguard the welfare of children and to bring the school, the home, and the community into closer cooperation.

C. Systematic interchange of professional knowledge, visits, and conferences through international organization and world education associations.

D. Teaching children the truth about war, its cost in human life and ideals, and in material wealth; the persistence of war in the history of all nations, the danger of its recurrence, and the need for effective international cooperation if future wars are to be avoided.

BIBLIOGRAPHY

American Association of School Administrators, N.E.A.: The Platform. 1201 Sixteenth Street, N.W., Washington, D.C. 1947.

American Association of School Administrators, N.E.A.: Report of the Resolutions Committee. 1201 Sixteenth Street, N.W., Washington, D.C. 1951.

Burton, William H.: The Guidance of Learning Activities. Appleton-Century Crofts. 1944.

Chamberlain & Kindred: The Teacher and School Administration. Prentice-Hall, Inc. 1950.

Council of State Governments: The Forty-eight State School Systems. Chicago, Ill. 1949.

Educational Policies Commission, National Education Association: The Purposes of Education in American Democracy. 1201 Sixteenth Street, N.W., Washington, D.C. 1938.

Educational Policies Commission, N.E.A.: Policies for Education in American Democracy. 1201 Sixteenth Street, N.W., Washington, D.C. 1946.

Educational Policies Commission, N.E.A.: Education for All American Children. 1201 Sixteenth Street, N.W., Washington, D.C. 1948.

Educational Policies Commission, N.E.A.: Moral and Spiritual Values in the Public Schools. 1201 Sixteenth Street, N.W., Washington, D.C. 1951.

Kilpatrick, William H.: The Education of Man (Aphorisms by Pestalozzi). Philosophical Library Inc., 15 East 40th Street, New York 16, New York, 1951.

Koopman, Meil, & Misner: Democracy in School Administration. D. Appleton-Century Co., 1943.

Law, Reuben D.: Content and Criteria Relating to Professional Teacher Education. University of Southern California. 1941.

National Education Association: Report of the Committee on Resolutions to the Representative Assembly. 1201 Sixteenth Street, N.W., Washington, D.C. 1948.

Remmlein, Madaline Kinter: School Law. McGraw-Hill. 1950.

Spears, Harold: Some Principles of Teaching. Prentice-Hall. 1951.

Utah State Department of Public Instruction, E. Allen Bateman, Superintendent: School Laws of the State of Utah. 1951.

Hughes and Lancelot: Education, America's Magic. Ames, Iowa, The Iowa State College Press. 1946.

U. S. Chamber of Commerce Committee on Education: Education, An Investment in People. Washington, D.C. 1944.

Wahlquist, John T.: An Introduction to American Education, Rev. New York, N.Y., Ronald Press. 1950.

Wahlquist, John T.: The Philosophy of American Education. New York, N.Y., Ronald Press. 1942.

CHAPTER II

SOME BACKGROUND INFLUENCES

A. *Religious Influence*

The importance of education for all the people was given strong support by the religious principles and doctrines espoused by the pioneers who settled the land which is now the State of Utah.

This settlement, beginning in 1847 and resulting from mass migrations of the leaders and membership of the Church of Jesus Christ of Latter-day Saints[1] provided a remarkable homogeneity of purposes and ideals seldom found among settlers of any land.

Until the coming of the railroad in 1869 there were very few settlers who were not of the L. D. S. faith, and even today the population of the state is approximately sixty-nine per cent L. D. S.[2]

The contributions of other groups who came and established or supported schools should, of course, be recognized and are appropriately mentioned in this volume.

In the three volumes of modern scripture[3], which, in addition to the bible, make up the officially adopted standard works of the church, there are at least one hundred twelve verses of scripture which make reference to education or to intelligence, learning, and wisdom in such a way as to be closely related to education and to educational philosophy. It is very significant that some of these references are in the form of divine commandment. Only a few of the above mentioned references are quoted here, but in the appendix[4] the reader may find a fuller listing of scriptural references to education:

---

1. Commonly called Mormons.
2. U. S. Census 1950 and L. D. S. Church Directory.
3. Doctrine and Covenants, Book of Mormon, and Pearl of Great Price.
4. Appendix A.

Seek not for riches but for wisdom. . .[5] (April, 1829).

And I give unto you a commandment that you shall teach one another. . . Teach ye diligently and my grace shall attend you that you may be instructed more perfectly. . . . in all things. . . . that are expedient for you to understand; of things both in heaven and in the earth, and under the earth; things which have been, things which are, things which must shortly come to pass; things which are at home, things which are abroad; the wars and the perplexities of the nations, and the judgments which are on the land; and a knowledge also of countries and kingdoms. . . .[6] (December 27, 1832).

. . . . seek ye diligently and teach one another words of wisdom; yea, seek ye out of the best books words of wisdom; seek learning, even by study and also by faith.[7]

Organize yourselves; prepart. . . a house of learning. . . . appoint among yourselves a teacher.[8] (Dec. 27, 1832).

. . . . study and learn and become acquainted with all good books, and with languages, tongues, and people.[9] (Dec. 27, 1832).

The glory of God is intelligence, or in other words, light and truth.[10] (May 6, 1833).

I have commanded you to bring up your children in light and truth.[11] (May 6, 1833).

And verily I say unto you that it is my will that you should. . . obtain a knowledge of history, and of countries, and of kingdoms, of laws of God and man. . .[12] (May 6, 1833).

5. Doctrine & Covenants, Sec. 6:7, also Sec. 11:7.
6. Ibid., Sec. 88:77-79.
7. Ibid., Sec. 88:118.
8. Ibid., Sec. 88:119 & 122
9. Ibid., Sec. 88:15.
10. Ibid., Sec. 93:36.
11. Ibid., Sec. 93:40.
12. Ibid., Sec. 93:53.

Go forward and not backward. . .[13] (Sept. 6, 1842).

Whatever principle of intelligence we attain unto in this life, it will rise with us in the resurrection. And if a person gains more knowledge and intelligence in this life through his diligence and obedience than another, he will have so much the advantage in the world to come.[14] (April 2, 1843).

It is impossible for a man to be saved in ignorance.[15] (May 16 or 17, 1843).

Let him that is ignorant learn wisdom.[16] (Jan. 14, 1847).

. . . To be learned is good if they hearken unto the counsels of God.[17]

If there is anything virtuous, lovely, or of good report or praiseworthy, we seek after these things.[18]

A people with such doctrines and beliefs, activated with the force of divine command and religious zeal and fervor, would be expected to give considerable attention to education for "all the children of all the people" and for adults as well. So evident has this been through the years that a United States Chamber of Commerce publication, based upon extensive investigations and research on education throughout the nation, carries the following statement: "Those of Mormon faith have been consistently strong proponents of education."[19]

A glance at the dates in parentheses following the scriptural quotations will support the assumption that the emphasis on education by this people began with the very early history of the church. During the seventeen years between 1830 and 1847 while the body of the church was

---

14. Ibid., Sec. 130:18 & 19.
15. Ibid., Sec. 131:6.
16. Ibid., Sec. 136:32.
17. Book of Mormon, Second Nephi 9:29.
18. Pearl of Great Price, Thirteenth Article of Faith. p. 58f.
19. Committee on Education, U. S. Chamber of Commerce: Education, An Investment in People, U. S. Chamber of Commerce Building, Washington, D. C., 1944.
13. Ibid., Sec. 128:22.

in the east and mid-west, schools were established for children and for adults. As early as June 1831, Oliver Cowdery and William W. Phelps were officially called to "the work of printing and of selecting and writing books for schools. . . . that little children may also receive instruction. . ."[20]

The school of the Prophets, which included children as well as adults, was organized at a very early date[21] and was later moved into the upper story of the Kirtland Temple wich was completed and dedicated in 1836.

In spite of difficulties associated with intense persecution in Missouri, the establishment of schools went forward there, also. Official church recognition and commendation was given to Parley P. Pratt in 1833 for his school work in Missouri.[22]

At Nauvoo, Illinois, under the authority of the Nauvoo Charter granted by the State of Illinois, a system of education was established, including a university. The University of the City of Nauvoo established under the leadership of Joseph Smith was both a university and an organization through which the schools of the community were organized and administered.

Even during the famous trek across the plains, groups were called together for study and instruction. The instructions of Brigham Young to his people in directing their preparation for the journey to the west carried items of educational significance.

For a more complete account of the educational efforts of the church and its people in the east and mid-west, and also in the far west, the reader is referred to Moffitt[23] and to Bennion.[24]

The first school in Utah was for a group of adults called together and instructed by George A. Smith who

---

20. Doctrine and Covenants, Sec. 55:4.
21. It is mentioned in the Doctrine and Covenants, Sec. 88, as early as 1832.
22. Doctrine and Covenants, Sec. 97:3-6.
23. Moffitt, J. C.: The History of Public Education in Utah. 1946.
24. Bennion, M. Lynn: Mormonism and Education, 1939.

had been especially active in teaching the children in the evenings during the trip from the middle west to the Salt Lake Valley.

The first school for children in Utah was taught in a tent by Mary Jane Dilworth shortly after the pioneers arrived in the valley of the Great Salt Lake in 1847.

President Brigham Young issued instructions to bishops directing them to provide a school in each ward. It is interesting to note that he had issued a similar edict in 1846 while at Council Bluffs by the Missouri River.

Wherever the people were sent to colonize the territory schools were immediately established. Almost invariably, one of the first buildings to be erected was a structure to be used for a school, for a church, and for recreation.

The community life arising from the Utah pioneer pattern of settling in villages and towns has been a very significant factor in the development of education.

The Territory of Utah was organized in 1850. Upon the recommendation of Governor Brigham Young in 1851 the Legislative Assembly authorized the chancellor and Board of Regents of the University of Deseret to appoint a "Superintendent of Primary Schools for the Territory of Utah." The 1852 Legislative Assembly created school districts. The development of the common schools as public schools under the control of school districts comprises a very significant and interesting story for which the reader may refer to Moffitt[25] and others.

Without going into detail it seems appropriate at this point to call attention to a very significant adherence to a great fundamental principle of American democracy in the very early separation of church and state in the legal control and financital support of the schools among a people so predominently of one religious faith. Of course

---

25. Moffitt, J. C.: The History of Public Education in Utah, 1946.

it was inevitably to be expected that many school trustees, teachers, and school administrators also held positions of responsibility in the church, but the legal demarcations and statutory provisions were clear and definite with respect to matters of separation of church and state in the operation and control of public schools by school districts.

From the very beginning there was careful safe-guarding of public school funds through provisions limiting their use to public schools only, leaving private schools to private support. This important principle was again re-emphasized in the following, quoted from a statute passed by the Utah Territorial Legislature in 1868:

> Nothing in this act nor in any former act shall be construed so as to appropriate any part of the public school funds to any private, select, or high school or any boarding school or academy, or any school whatever not under the immediate control and direction of the school district trustees.[26]

This becomes all the more significant when it is called to mind that history records many examples in other states and other nations where strong predominent religious groups of certain other faiths have held tenaciously to the control of the schools by the church, and have insisted upon public tax funds for the support of parochial schools. Today in the United States there are some states in which public school moneys raised through public taxation are still apportioned regularly to parochial schools.[27]

Just as elementary schools were fostered by the church until territorial school districts were provided to operate the common schools, so also did the church provide institutions for secondary and college education until such time as consolidated school districts and the state were able and willing to render this service. The church

---

26. Territorial Laws of Utah, 1868.
27. This issue flared up in a very troublesome way in relation to proposed congression appropriations to the states for general federal aid to education.

then turned a number of these institutions over to the
state as a gift for the specified sum of one dollar to make
the transaction legal and binding, with the provision that
the property was to be used by the state for educational
institutions.

Beginning in 1875 with the Brigham Young Academy, L. D. S. Church Academies were established in many
places over the intermountain west. Table I contains a
list of these academies with the year of opening, and the
location of each.[28]

Table I

Academies Established by the church of Jesus Christ of
Latter-day Saints[29]

Name	Year Opened	Location
Brigham Young Academy	1875	Provo, Utah
Salt Lake Stake Academy	1886	Salt Lake City, Utah
Fielding Academy	1887	Paris, Idaho
Ricks Academy	1888	Rexberg, Idaho
Snow Academy	1888	Ephraim, Utah
Oneida Stake Academy	1888	Preston, Idaho
Snowflake Academy	1888	Snowflake, Arizona
St. Johns Academy	1888	St. Johns, Arizona
Uintah Stake Academy	1888	Vernal, Utah
Cassia Stake Academy	1889	Oakley, Idaho
Weber Academy	1889	Ogden, Utah
Emery Academy	1890	Castle Dale, Utah
Gila Academy	1891	Thatcher, Arizona
Juarez Academy	1897	Colonia Juarez, Mexico
Murdock Academy	1898	Beaver, Utah
San Luis Academy	1905	Sanford, Colorado
Summit Academy	1906	Coalville, Utah
Big Horn Academy	1909	Cowley, Wyoming
Millard Academy	1910	Hinckley, Utah
Knight Academy	1910	Raymond, Alberta, Canada
Dixie Academy	1911	St. George, Utah

28. Data supplied by Dr. Franklin L. West, Church Commissioner of
    Education.
29. A list of L. D. S. educational institutions is given in Bennion, M. Lynn:
    Mormonism and Education, p. 164.

Most of these academies became the forerunners of modern public high schools with the blossoming of the high school movement and the consolidation of school districts into units large enough to establish and maintain high schools. A number of the academies developed into colleges and universities.

Brigham Young College was founded at Logan, Utah, in 1877 with a generous endowment of land, by President Brigham Young. The school flourished until 1926 when it was closed to divert use of the funds for its maintenance to the establishment and maintenance of church seminaries and institutes.

Brigham Young Academy, Provo, Utah, developed into Brigham Young University.

Salt Lake Stake Academy was changed during the third year of its operation to Latter-day Saints' College. In June, 1931, the high school and junior college divisions of the school were discontinued, and the institution has since operated as the L. D. S. Business College.[30] In 1952 this institution became a branch of Brigham Young University.

The McCune School of Music and Art, Salt Lake City, had its beginning in the Music Department of the L. D. S. University. The school became located in the Gardo House in 1919 and was known as the L. D. S. School of Music. In 1920 it moved into the McCune Mansion and its name was changed to the L. D. S. McCune School of Music and Art.[31]

Ricks Academy at Rexberg, Idaho, became Ricks College, now a degree granting four year college. Snow Academy, which was founded as Sanpete Stake Academy developed into Snow College at Ephraim, Utah. In 1951 this school became a branch of the Utah State Agricultural

---

30. Gold and Blue, Special Edition, Founders' Day, November 15, 1950,
    L. D. S. Business College, Salt Lake City.
31. Information supplied by Iola Hoggan, Secretary, from an article written
    by Tracy Y. Cannon.

College. Weber Academy at Ogden became Weber College. Gila Academy became Gila College at Thatcher, Arizona, now Eastern Arizona Junior College, and Dixie Academy developed into Dixie College, St. George, Utah. With the exception of Ricks, the institutions mentioned in this paragraph were later turned over to the state school systems of the states in which they are located.

In the 1920's and early '30's, with the exception of Brigham Young University, Ricks College, L. D. S. Business College, McCune School of Music and Art, Juarez Stake Academy, and Mission Schools in several parts of the world, the L. D. S. church withdrew from high school and college secular instruction and has established a system of church seminaries and institutes, located on church property in close proximity to high schools, colleges, and universities.

The extensive emphasis on elementary and secondary education and on college and university work by this church group has been a remarkably potent and far-reaching factor in the development of education in Utah and wherever groups of L. D. S. people have settled.

The educational efforts and accomplishments of other church groups of other religious faiths should also be recognized. The development of schools by church groups other than L. D. S. came after the completion of the railroad from east to west in 1869. According to Dr. LeRoy E. Cowles[32] there were several denominational schools established in the territory between 1870 and 1875. Previously, one school which soon ceased to exist was opened in 1867. Six such schools employing twenty-nine teachers were reported in 1874 by the U. S. Commissioner of Education. In 1875, when there were 18,278 pupils enrolled in the territorial public schools, 1,699 pupils were enrolled in the denominational schools.

---

32. Cowles, LeRoy E.: Organization and Administration of Public Education in Utah. 1949.

Wasatch Academy in Mt. Pleasant was founded in 1875 and Logan Academy in 1878. The corner stone of Saint Mary's Academy, Salt Lake City, was laid in 1875 and in 1926 the name of the school was changed to the College and Academy of Saint Mary of the Wasatch. The Sacred Heart Academy at Ogden was established in 1878. Rowland Hall, Salt Lake City, began in 1880. Salt Lake Collegiate Institute was founded in 1875 and was later merged with Westminster College which was founded in 1897. All Hallows College provided instruction between 1885 and 1918 at Salt Lake City. Other denominational schools are Judge Memorial High School and Elementary School, Salt Lake City; Notre Dame (Elementary and Junior High), Price, Utah; St. Joseph's School, Ogden (Elementary and Junior High); Cathedral School, Salt Lake City; St. Ann's School, Salt Lake City; St. John's Lutheran School, Salt Lake City.

According to Dr. Cowles,[33] in 1948-49 the total enrollment of Catholic and Protestant schools in Utah was approximately 2,522.

B. *Civic Mindedness*

The programs of positive support by many civic and professional groups, too numerous to mention by name, have also added materially to the continuous interest in education shown by the people of Utah.

As indicated in Chapter I, it has long been recognized that educated citizens are much more likely to develop attitudes and practices of civic interest and responsibility than are people among whom education has been neglected. In this respect it is significant to note that Utah leads all other states of the U. S. in the percentage of those voting at elections. The following is quoted from a recent report on voting in national elections:[34]

---

33. Ibid.
34. Deseret News, April 11, 1949. p. B.8.

The best voting record in both 1948 and 1944 national elections was made by the people of Utah. This is disclosed in a statistical report made by Sen. Owen Brewster (R-Me.), who suggests that it might be that the people of the United States who do not vote decide national elections.

According to statistics gathered by Senator Brewster ,who is chairman of the senatorial campaign committee, only 52 per cent of those eligible in the U. S. voted in the 1948 national election, and only 59 per cent voted in the 1944 election. Out of 93,-704,000 eligible voters, 44,870,320 failed to cast ballots in 1948; and out of 80,298,000 eligible, 32,-321, 737 failed to vote in 1944. . . .

In 1948, 74.6 per cent of the eligible voters in Utah voted. . . . In 1944, 79.3 per cent of the voting population. . . . voted.

Of course, it is regrettable that 25.4 per cent and 20.7 per cent of Utahns eligible to vote failed to go to the polls in the national elections of 1948 and 1944 respectively, but relatively speaking the record is strikingly superior to the average for the nation. It is to be hoped that the near future will show a desirable increase in both national and state voting percentages.

There are many things to which attention could be drawn as possible evidences of civic interest and responsibility or the lack of it. Perhaps the reader would like to list some of these, being careful to correctly and objectively check the facts upon which his conclusions may be based.

It is at least interesting to note that the state with the highest voting record also ranks highest in the nation in the average amount of schooling completed by the adult population[35] and ranks among the four states with the lowest amount of consumption of distilled spirits per capita.[36]

C. *The Westward Movement*

To many the westward movement among a freedom loving people with its accompanying emphasis on individual resourcefulness and the worth of the individual person, and with the development of attitudes and practices which have enhanced our concepts of democracy, has itself been an influence of no small proportions in relation to the development of education in this area.

Many of the writings of reputable historians in the field of western history appear to give some credence at least to this point of view.

D. *Consolidation*

A very important development which has contributed significantly to education in Utah is the early consolidation of school districts into administrative units of sufficient size to favor the operation of schools with a high degree of efficiency and professionalism. By 1915 the schools of Utah had been organized into only forty school districts. With a moderate expenditure of school funds per pupil, the state has been among the leading states in educational achievement as the next section of this chapter will show.

It seems evident that this early trend toward consolidation of school districts was influenced by the type of eclesiastical organization to which the people were accustomed in their religious activities. The organization of groups of wards (local church units of organization) into stakes as units of L. D. S. church administration, comprising a sizeable area, brought people together from quite a

35. U. S Census Bureau; Also Hughes & Lancelot: Education America's Magic. p. 12. Iowa State College Press. 1946.
36. Distilled Spirits Institute, Inc., Washington, D. C.

number of communities to quarterly stake conferences and monthly to union meetings or conventions. Furthermore, stake officials traveled over the area supervising the work of the church and participating in meetings of the local wards. People were thus accustomed to thinking in terms of larger geographic areas of cooperation as they actively participated with those of other communities. It is significant to note that when Salt Lake County consolidated into two districts in 1904, those two districts (Granite and Jordan) were organized with exactly the same boundaries, and also adopted the same names, as the two L. D. S. stakes which were at that time operating in the Salt Lake Valley outside of Salt Lake City.

The influence of territorial and state superintendents of schools in favoring larger school districts should also be recognized as well as that of other educational leaders of the territory and the state. School reports of the time make repeated reference to this matter.[37 and 38]

There is considerable evidence pointing to the conclusion that Utah's system of consolidation has been an important factor in the educational development and in the efficiency of the schools of this state.

E. *Some Evidences of Educational Accomplishment*

A word of caution is appropriate before presenting the material for the remainder of this chapter. This material is given in a spirit of deep humility and grateful appreciation, and in no sense should it be interpreted in an attitude of smugness or complacency or with the mistaken assumption that these people have "arrived" with no further need for improvement, and might safely coast for a while. The very nature of education calls for continuous improvement and continuous effort in the meeting of new challenges. There is undoubtedly need for

---

37. Territorial and State School Reports.
38. Moffitt, J. C.: The History of Public Education in Utah. 1946.

greater attention to the best possible educational effort than ever before. Any attitude or practice of complacency is dangerous and can rapidly result in loss of ground, painstakingly gained through the intelligent and faithful struggles of a people and its leadership over a period of many years. The reader will be familiar with President Thomas Jefferson's oft quoted statement that, "Eternal vigilence is the price of liberty." Likewise, eternal vigilence and never ending effort in the light of continuous re-evaluation is the price of good education among any people.

Almost invariably, when objective studies of education in the United States have been made in such a way as to show the relative status of the various states of the union the state of Utah has been placed in a rather favorable position. Reference will here be made to a sufficient number of such studies to rule out the possibility of impressions which might have arisen from sporadic or chance selection by the investigators.

Under the caption, "Utah Leads the Nation in Education," a Deseret News editorial made reference to a U. S. Office of Education report as follows:

Some interesting figures have just been released by the National Education Association showing the rating of this state in the nation from an educational standpoint. Some of those statistics are rather astounding, and are apt to astonish the most loyal Utahn even. For it is shown among other things that in the school year 1941-42 there were 15 high school graduates for every 1000 population, or a total of 8,253. . . . The national average was 8.83. These statistics were compiled from data supplied by the U. S. Office of Education and the U. S. Bureau of the census.

Other tables released disclose that the median years of school completed by citizens of Utah over 25 years of age are 10.2 placing this state at the head of the nation in this category. . . . The average for the United States was 8.4 years.

The daily cost of educating each student in Utah is given as $0.4868. . . . The national average is $0.563. [39]

Eight years earlier there had appeared in the public press a report of an extensive survey by Schrammel and Sonnenbry: [40]

A gratifying compliment is paid to the educational efficiency of the Utah school system in a recent survey of all the states, made for the purpose of ranking the states educationally. This extensive survey was by H. E. Schrammel and E. R. Sonnenbry, the former director of the Bureau of Educational Measurements, Kansas State Teachers' College, and the latter superintendent of schools of Coyville, Kansas.

The rank of the states, according to educational achievement is on the basis of the following eleven selected criteria:

1. The length of the school term in average number of days the schools were in session.

2. The per cent of the total population enrolled in public elementary and secondary schools.

3. The per cent of the school population, 5 to 18 years of age, enrolled in the public schools.

4. The per cent of pupils enrolled who were in average daily attendance.

5. The per cent that public secondary school enrollment is of the total public school enrollment.

6. The per cent of those enrolled who graduate from public secondary schools.

---

39. Deseret News Editorial, October 15, 1944; These data are, of course, also available through the National Education Association and the U. S. Office of Education.
40. Deseret News, November, 1936.

7. The per cent of the total population ten years and over that is literate.

8. The per cent of illiteracy eliminated during the preceding decade.

9. The amount expended for education per capita of total population.

10. The amount expended for education per pupil in average daily attendance.

11. The amount expended for education per $1,000 of estimated true value of all property.

The data for computing the rank of the various states on the individual criteria were obtained from the U. S. Office of Education. . . .

While these eleven criteria do not establish absolute standing in educational efficiency, any one at all familiar with the aims of education cannot but accept them as factors of the greatest significance in estimating the rank of the state in education.

The fact that Utah ranks second of the forty-eight states in this survey is a distinct compliment to our educators and to the public in general. It should serve to inspire even greater efforts on the part of school officials and school patrons toward the solution of the important educational problems still confronting us.

The Education Committee of the United States Chamber of Commerce conducted a series of extensive statistical studies, showing a significant relationship between good education and good business prosperity over the United States as a whole, the results of which were published in a volume entitled, "Education, An Investment in People"[41] Table XII-A, page 33, gives the median years of schooling completed by persons twenty years of age and over in

41. Education Committee, U. S. Chamber of Commerce: Education, An Investment in People. U. S. Chamber of Commerce Building, Washington, D. C., 1944.

each state in 1940 with Utah in first place among the states with a median of 10.8 compared with 8.8 for the United States.

Page 48 of this same publication carries the statement that "Utah has been out in front among the sparsely settled states with an exceptionally good basic educational organization. . ."

According to the results of a Harvard committee's two year survey, as reported in Salt Lake City by Dr. Paul H. Buck[42] in 1946, Utah was rated one of the two highest states for education in the United States.

An investigation for the Veterans Administration was published by the Salt Lake Tribune[43] under the caption "Utah Education Facilities for Vets Top Nation, Ratio of School Attendance Surpasses all other States":

Utah is better prepared than any other state in the nation to provide adequate higher education facilities for its returning veterans.

This was pointed out by Dr. S. E. Partch, school of education dean, Rutgers University, New Brunswick, New Jersey, whose recently completed survey of national education needs was received Tuesday. . .

Utah also ranks first in the number of persons per 10,000 population attending educational institutions.

The number of persons of secondary school age per 10,000 population in Utah attending school is 775, compared to a national average of 510.

In the pre-war year 1939-40, Utah had 151 men and 86 women students (total 237) per 10,000 population in higher educational institutions, compared with a national average of 112 students. Nearest state to Utah in per capita college attend-

---

42. Salt Lake Tribune, February 27, 1946.
43. Ibid.

ance was California with 174 students. In Delaware only 42 persons per 10,000 population were attending college in 1939-40.

The editor of the publication, "American Men of Science," Dr. Cattell, found by actual tabulation that, in relation to population, there were more eminent scientists listed with birth places in Utah than in any other state. He commented about this to his professional colleague, Dr. Edward L. Thorndike, who immediately wondered if this might or might not be true of people in positions of eminence generally. He, therefore, directed a study of birth places listed for people who had been included in recent editions of "Who's Who in America," "Leaders in Education," and "American Men of Science." Dr. Thorndike's results prompted the following quotation from a newspaper article:[44]

Utah Shares Top Rank for Brains

If there were some sort of Rose Bowl contest between states that produce the most smart people per 1,000,000 population, the nod would go to Utah and Massachusetts. At least so says a report filed. . . . with the American Academy of Sciences by Professor Edward L. Thorndike, Columbia University psychologist. He listed those states in one-two order with respect to producing "men and women of great ability."

A very extensive comparative study of education in all the states, and also involving data from 109 nations of the world, was authored in 1946 by Raymond M. Hughes and William H. Lancelot, a college president emeritus and a professor of education at Iowa State College.[45]

The forty-eight states were rated on (1) accomplish-

---

44. Salt Lake Tribune, December 8, 1940.
45. Hughes & Lancelot: Education, America's Magic. State College of Iowa Press. Ames, Iowa. 1946.

ment in education, (2) their ability to support education, (3) the degree in which their accomplishment is commensurate with their ability, (4) on the degree of effort of the states to provide for education, (5) on the efficiency of their educational effort, and (6) on the educational level of the adult population. Also, an all-round educational rank was obtained. For the specifics as to what was included in the measurement of each of these items, the reader should refer to the publication itself. The reader will also be especially interested in the summary tables found on pages 12, 47, 48, 49, 51, 63, 73, 77, 78, and 85 which provide a very useful array of significant data.

In a chapter entitled "Balance Sheet of the States" the authors of the publication have provided a summary statement regarding each of the states. The summary pertaining to Utah is here quoted:[46]

> Utah has first place among the states by a wide margin. It outranks Oregon in accomplishment by 5.5 per cent. It excells Kansas in the difference between actual and expected accomplishment by 11.9 points (Table 6). It excels Nebraska in the scale of efficiency by 6.9 points (Table 9). Its adult citizens on the average have 0.24 year more education than do the citizens of California (Table 10).

> While ranking 32 in (financial)ability to support education with an income of only $1,680 per child, and 4 in effort, it still ranks first in educational accomplishment, (first) in the degree in which accomplishment is commensurate with ability, (first) in efficiency, and (first) in the level of adult education.

> This appears to be due almost wholly to the high value placed on education by the people of Utah, coupled with high efficiency in the expenditure of

---

46. Ibid., pp. 40 and 41.

funds devoted to school purposes. Indeed, the combination of great effort and high efficiency in the utilization of school funds seems to have operated in a remarkable manner to overcome the handicap of relatively low (financial) ability.

Utah easily outclasses all other states in over-all performance in education.

The data provided regarding the 109 nations are extremely interesting, showing that no other nation provides as much education for as large a percentage of its population as does the United States, and certainly thinking people are aware of the need for much improvement in this respect in the United States. An awareness of the principle that an enlightened populace is essential to progress toward peace in the world leaves one with the realization that much remains to be done. It is most regrettable that the data reveal sixty-four nations[47] in which less than fifty per cent of the children between six and thirteen years of age are enrolled in school.

Tables II, III, and IV list the top twenty-five nations in elementary school enrollment, secondary school enrollment, and college enrollment respectively.

Table II.
Per Cent of Those 6-13 Enrolled in Elementary Schools

1.	Australia	119.6	14.	British Honduras	87.0
2.	United States	119.5	15.	Bulgaria	85.5
3.	France	114.8	16.	Greece	85.5
4.	Canada	113.0	17.	Czechoslovakia	83.8
5.	New Zealand	111.0	18.	Germany	83.4
6.	Great Britain	104.3	19.	Sweden	82.0
7.	Eire (South Ireland)	103.0	20.	Argentina	81.0
8.	Denmark	102.0	21.	Italy	76.7
9.	Russia	99.0	22.	Japan	75.8
10.	Belgium	92.5	23.	Norway	74.8
11.	Switzerland	92.3	24.	Finland	73.8
12.	Poland	91.6	25.	Yugoslavia	69.4
13.	Netherlands	88.8			

47. Ibid., p. 185.

Table III.

Per Cent of Those 14-17 Enrolled in Secondary Schools

1.	United States	63.6*	14.	Australia	21.1
2.	Canada	55.8	15.	Yugoslavia	21.1
3.	Belgium	55.7	16.	Finland	20.4
4.	Great Britain	50.8	17.	Chile	20.1
5.	Japan	45.5	18.	Bulgaria	19.9
6.	Denmark	44.3	19.	Italy	19.5
7.	Germany	43.5	20.	Poland	17.7
8.	Czechoslovakia	43.3	21.	Eire (South Ireland)	17.0
9.	Switzerland	42.6	22.	Sweden	15.9
10.	Netherlands	40.9	23.	Norway	14.3
11.	France	33.5	24.	Panama	14.2
12.	Russia	32.9	25.	Uruguay	13.9
13.	New Zealand	27.9			

*Reported by Allen to be 81.2 per cent by 1947.[48]

Table IV.

Per Cent of Those 18-21 Enrolled in Colleges and Universities

1.	United States	14.65*	14.	Germany	3.04
2.	Uruguay	9.25	15.	Denmark	2.95
3.	Australia	8.5	16.	Bulgaria	2.92
4.	Canada	6.17	17.	Eire (South Ireland)	2.72
5.	Russia	6.00	18.	France	2.62
6.	New Zealand	5.63	19.	Czechoslovakia	2.52
7.	Cuba	4.17	20.	Argentina	2.50
8.	Switzerland	3.84	21.	Paraguay	2.49
9.	Belgium	3.64	22.	Norway	2.36
10.	Great Britain	3.61	23.	Italy	2.25
11.	Finland	3.36	24.	Palestine	2.16
12.	Japan	3.19	25.	Sweden	2.08[49]
13.	Mexico	3.09			

*Had increased remarkably beyond this percentage by 1950.

A veritable treasure house of data regarding the schools of the various states is provided in a recent publication by the Council of State Governments, with Francis

---

48. Allen: The Federal Government and Education. p. 9. McGraw-Hill Co. 1950.
49. For the rest of the nations see Hughes and Lancelot, p. 185.

S. Chase as Director of Research and Edgar L. Morphet as Associate Director of the study.[50]

Bearing in mind the relatively high accomplishments already noted, it is interesting to observe from chart 8, dealing with current expense per pupil in average daily attendance, that, as of the school year 1947-48, Utah stood in twenty-first position in the cost per pupil in A.D.A.[51]

The state ranks among the top five states in the preparation of its teachers, with 76.1 per cent holding bachelor's or master's degrees or higher, including the necessary work in professional education as of the school year 1947-48.[52] With the relatively large graduating classes in the schools and colleges of education during recent years this percentage should be considerably higher at the present time. Also, the state is favorably recognized for the organization of its teacher education program in its colleges and universities.[53] Another evidence of professionalism is the fact that for years this state has ranked in the number one position in the percentage of its teachers who are members of the National Education Association.

As an outcome of some phases of the progress in school organization referred to earlier, Utah is one of two states with the smallest number of one teacher schools; also ,one of two with the smallest percentage of one teacher schools.[54]

Such a vast array of tables are provided carrying statistical data on various aspects of education that an attempt will not be mde to summarize them here, but the reader is encouraged to refer to this useful volume.[55]

---

50. Council of State Governments: The Forty-eight State School Systems. Council of State Governments, Chicago, Illinois, 1949.
51. Ibid., pp. 24, 178, and 179.
52. Ibid., pp. 71 and 202.
53. Ibid. See Kansas material.
54. Ibid., pp. 56, 57, and 194.
55. Ibid.

F. *What of the Future?*

The people of a state with such a heritage, and with such sincere and far-reaching purposes for fostering education, would be expected to achieve a position of leadership educationally. In the years ahead will they continue to do so, or will short sighted opposition or complacency permit a decline in relative standing among the states? Leadership carries with it sobering obligations to society in this state or any other state or nation.

The achievements of the past did not just happen. They resulted from planning and from persistent, intelligent effort to bring about improvement in organization, in educational offering, in buildings, and conditions, and from struggles to procure needed revenues by people of courage, inspiration, and vision. These struggles must continue with renewed energy and determination; the forces of selfishness and error must be more effectively opposed by an educationally minded citizenry and its leadership, with a constructive, far-reaching program of progress. Those who have worked in the program know that the forces of opposition and error have been busy in the past, and there cannot be envisioned a time in the forseeable future when such forces will not have to be opposed.

Remember that because eternal vigilence is the price of liberty it is therefore also the price of good education in a democracy. What of the future?

BIBLIOGRAPHY

Bennion, M. Lynn: Mormonism and Education. Department of Education of the Church of Jesus Christ of Latter-day Saints. 1939, Salt Lake City, Utah

Book of Mormon. 1830, (also later editions) Deseret Book Company, Salt Lake City, Utah.

Butts, R. F.: The American Tradition in Religion and Education. The Beacon Press, Boston, 1950.

Childs, J. L.: Education and Morals. Appleton-Century-Crofts, 1950.

Council of State Governments: The Forty-Eight State School Systems. Chicago, Illinois. 1949.

Doctrine and Covenants of the Church of Jesus Christ of Latter-day Saints. 1833, 1835, (also later editions) Deseret Book Co. Salt Lake City, Utah.

History of the Church, Vols. 1 to 7.

Hughes and Lancelot: Education, America's Magic. State College of Iowa Press. Ames, Iowa. 1946.

Moffitt, J. C.: The History of Public Education in Utah. 1946. Chapter 1 ff.

Pearl of Great Price. 1835, 1902, 1921. Deseret Book Company, Salt Lake City.

U. S. Chamber of Commerce Committee on Education: Education, An Investment in People. Chamber of Commerce Building, Washington, D. C. 1944.

CHAPTER III

DESCRIPTIVE OVERVIEW OF
EDUCATIONAL ORGANIZATION

*Education
a State
Function*
Education is essentially a state function. The organization and control of education are not mentioned in the federal constitution, but are left to the states where the subject of education is necessarily and definitely mentioned in the various state constitutions.[1] The federal government, however, does perform functions in relation to education. These are discussed in Chapter XII.

As viewed within the state, education is essentially a state function, the sovereignty for which rests with the people of the entire state and not automatically and independently with the residents of each separate hamlet or local community.

*Legal Basis
for School
System*
The people of the entire area comprising what is now the state of Utah elected and sent representatives to a constitutional convention charged with the responsibility of preparing a state constitution according to the desires of the people and in line with the constitution of the United States and the federal statutes. This constitution was adopted by the people of the state and approved by the Congress of the United States in passing the enabling act in 1895 which admitted Utah to the Union in January of 1896.

This constitution, with subsequent state law, provides the legal basis for the organization and operation of the public school system of Utah. The school system was defined in the constitution and, with certain exceptions, the

---

1. This statement is not made in opposition to federal aid to education. There is evidence of great need for federal aid in the financially poorer states, but the control of education should be left with the states.

details of specific school law were wisely left to the legislature. Sections 1 and 2 of Article X are here quoted as follows:

Article X

Education

Section 1. (Free non-sectarian schools).

The Legislature shall provide for the establishment and maintenance of a uniform system of public schools, which shall be open to all children of the state, and be free from sectarian control.

Section 2. (Defining what shall constitute the public school system).

The public school system shall include kindergarten schools; common schools, consisting of primary and grammar grades; high schools; an agricultural college; a university; and such other schools as the Legislature may establish. The common schools shall be free. The other departments of the system shall be supported as provided by law. (As amended November 8, 1910.)[2]

Subsequent state law provides that, "In each school district the public schools shall be free to all children between the ages of six and eighteen years who are residents of said districts." With the inclusion of kindergarten in the public schools the five year olds were also included. Any tuition charges in the public elementary or secondary schools of Utah would, therefore, be illegal.

State Board of Education Superintendent, and Staff
As indicated in Section 8 of Article X, quoted below, the constitution provided for a state board of education with general control and supervision of all public schools:

---

2. Utah Code Annotated 1943, Vol. 1, pp. 144, 145.

Section 8. (State Board of Education).

The general control and supervision of the Public school System shall be vested in a State Board of Education, consisting of the Superintendent of Public Instruction, and such other persons as the Legislature may provide.[3]

This section was amended by vote of the people in November, 1950, to read as follows:[4]

"Sec. 8. The general control and supervision of the public school system shall be vested in a State Board of Education the members of which shall be elected as provided by law.

The Board shall appoint the State Superintendent of Public Instruction who shall be the executive officer of the Board."[5]

The State Superintendent of Public Instruction, with the approval of the State Board of Education, selects assistant state superintendents and members of the State School Office staff. For the present personnel makeup of the membership of the State Board of Education, the State Superintendent, assistant superintendents, and staff, the reader is referred to the current issue of the Utah Public School Directory:[6] The details of organization, powers, duties, and responsibilities of the state school organization are treated in Chapter IV.

*School Districts
As Arms of
the State*
The local school districts, in which the work of the elementary and secondary schools is carried on, are arms of the state, created by legislative enactment based on constitutional mandate and authority, and are not local subdivisions of city and county governments. District boards of education and their appointed officials

---

3. **Ibid.,** p. 147.
4. Prior to this time the State Superintendent of Public Instruction was elected at the regular November election.
5. School Laws of the State of Utah, 1951.
6. Utah Public School Directory, State Department of Public Instruction, Salt Lake City, Utah (most recent issue).

derive their authority from state law, and are directly responsible to the people on a strictly non partisan basis. When the local people go to the polls on the first Wednesday in December and elect members of district boards of education they are acting under state authority provided by legislative enactment. This legislative enactment was by representatives of the people of the entire state in line with the provisions of the constitution.

Forty School Districts The state is organized into forty school districts[7] five of which are city school districts and thirty-five of which are consolidated school districts most of which are coextensive in area with the counties in which they are located. There are twenty-nine counties in the state,[8] but as noted above there are thirty-five consolidated school districts outside the cities of the first and second class. The reason for having more consolidated districts than there are counties in the state is really an historical one. Prior to the compulsory consolidation legislation of 1915, much of the state had voluntarily consolidated under the permissive consolidation legislation of 1905[9] and earlier (liberalized in 1911 and 1913), and in some counties more than one consolidated school district had already been organized.

Consolidation Provision was made for recognizing these districts when the legislation was written in 1915. The growth of high schools influenced this development. The law that was enacted in 1915 provided that in counties having a school population of 5000 or more and already divided into two or more high school districts each such high school district was to constitute a consolidated district of the first class.

Accordingly, the counties in which two or more consolidated districts were recognized are Salt Lake (Granite

7. See figure 1.
8. See figure 1.
9. See Moffitt: The History of Public Education in Utah, 1946 (Chapter XII)

and Jordan districts), Utah (Alpine and Nebo districts), Sanpete (North Sanpete and South Sanpete districts), Summit (North Summit, South Summit, and Park City districts), and Juab (Juab and Tintic districts). In all other counties one consolidated school district comprises the entire area of the county outside of cities of the first- and second-class.

Following some combining of small districts under permissive legislation in territorial days, the first consolidations affecting entire counties under statehood occurred in Salt Lake County (December, 1904, which was prior to the 1905 legislation), Weber County (July 3, 1905), and Box Elder (May, 1907).[10] By 1912 Cache, Morgan, Davis, and Sevier had been added to this group,[11] and before 1915 Uintah County had consolidated.

Section 6 of Article X of the State constitution provides that "In cities of the first and second class the public school system shall be controlled by the Board of Education of such cities, separate and apart from the counties in which said cities are located" (as amended November 6, 1900).[12]

The five city districts are in Salt Lake City, Ogden, Provo, Logan, and Murray. For the history of the development of these city districts during the territorial period of Utah's history the reader is referred to Moffitt's interesting treatment of this subject.[13]

*District
Organization*
In each of the forty school districts the board of education, elected by the people, appoints a superintendent of schools. The superintendent is the executive officer of the board and serves as the professional head of the school system of the district. Lest there be confusion in the mind of the reader,

10. **Ibid.,** page 213.
11. **Ibid.,** page 214.
12. Utah Code Annotated 1943, Vol. 1, p. 147.
13. Moffitt: The History of Public Education in Utah, 1946, pp. 208 ff.
14. In the absence of the president from meetings, the vice president is the presiding officer of the board.

it should be noted that the president of the board is the presiding officer of the board of education,[14] and the superintendent, who is appointed by and is responsible to the board, is the chief executive officer of the board of education with the responsibility of making recommendations to the board and of carrying out or executing the decisions of the board with the help of the employees of the district.

In each of these districts there are elementary (including kindergarten) and secondary (junior high and senior high) schools. In a typical district there are a number of elementary schools, several junior high schools, and one or more senior high schools with a principal in charge of each school, responsible to the superintendent and through him to the board of education. This arrangement makes possible the advantages that accrue from having the education of children and youth from kindergarten to and through the twelfth grade coordinated under the unifying administration and supervision of a sizeable school district under one board of education. There are also advantages related to efficiency of operation and the use of school funds.

Approximately 21,528 of the elementary pupils and 24,658 of the secondary pupils were transported in school buses from their homes or points near their homes to and from school daily in the year 1950-51.

Adult Education — Adult education opportunities are also provided for the adults of the various communities.

As indicated in the preceding chapter, this system of consolidation of school districts and consolidation of schools within districts appears to be one of the very significant factors in the development of an efficient and

widely recognized modern program of education in this
state.[15]

It should be emphasized that a very desirable, high
type of community life, with close inter-relationships between school and community, is highly important, especially in a democracy. The school has been and will continue to be an important community center, and likewise
the community life in this state, with intercommunity relationships, has been a stimulating factor in the development of good schools. For the interesting history of the
development of these schools, the reader is again referred
to Moffitt[16] and to Cowles.[17]

Attention is called to the fact that the citizenry of
Utah during an earlier period lived for a time under a
system in which there were large numbers of very small
school districts as units of local school administration, with
a board of three school trustees in each little hamlet or
small local area. These trustees in each separate community, or part of a town in some cases, levied the taxes
on the property within the district, purchased the supplies, hired the teacher, etc. To check on these many
small districts and perform certain duties there was an
elected county superintendent of schools. At the time
Utah became a state in 1896, such a system, being generally in vogue over a large part of the country, was adopted
by our legislators in formulating the basic school law.

However, the seeds of consolidation to provide for
improved school organization had already been planted in
fertile soil and they continued to sprout and grow with
amazing rapidity. In addition to their experience during
Utah's territorial existence, it took the people, under for-

---

15. A larger percentage of the population graduate from high school each
    year than in any other state or nation. Also, a larger percentage of the
    population attend colleges and universities than is the case in any other
    state or nation. In average number of years of schooling completed by
    the adult population, Utah ranks first or highest. (See Hughes and
    Lancelot: Education, America's Magic.)
16. Moffitt: The History of Public Education in Utah, 1946.
17. Cowles: Organization and Administration of Public Education in Utah,
    1949.

ward looking leadership, only nineteen short years after being admitted to the union as a state to achieve a system of school district consolidation with the entire state organized into only forty school districts and with each school district under a single board of education with the professional services of an appointed superintendent of schools.

School Districts in the Forty-Eight States   A recent publication by the Council of State Governments[18] provides some interesting data regarding the number of school districts in each of the forty-eight states. These data are given in Table V.

Table V
Number of School Districts in the Forty-Eight States, 1947-48[19]

State	Total No. of Districts	State	Total No. of Districts
Alabama	108	Nevada	222
Arizona	325	New Hampshire	239
Arkansas	1,589	New Jersey	561
California	2,349	New Mexico	497
Colorado	1,794	New York	4,609
Connecticut	174	North Carolina	172
Delaware	126	North Dakota	2,271
Florida	67	Ohio	1,539
Georgia	189	Oklahoma	2,669
Idaho	648	Oregon	1,363
Illinois	11,061*	Pennsylvania	2,540
Indiana	1,191	Rhode Island	39
Iowa	4,709	South Carolina	1,680
Kansas	5,643	South Dakota	3,409
Kentucky	246	Tennessee	150
Louisiana	67	Texas	4,832
Maine	493	Utah	40
Maryland	24	Vermont	268
Massachusetts	351	Virginia	125
Michigan	5,434*	Washington	584
Minnesota	7,518	West Virginia	55
Mississippi	4,211	Wisconsin	6,385*
Missouri	8,422	Wyoming	354
Montana	1,512		
Nebraska	6,864	All states	99,713

* 1946-47 data.

18. The Forty-Eight State School Systems. Council of State Governments, Chicago, Illinois, 1949. Table 18, page 192.

Further consolidation of districts in some parts of the State of Utah may still be desirable. For example, the three relatively small districts in Summit County might very well be organized into one school district. Other consolidations would also seem to be desirable. Extensive proposals have been made by Dr. George H. Hansen, Dr. Amos N. Merrill and others regarding further reorganization, and additional proposals will undoubtedly be considered in the future.

Character Education and School-Community Relations   From the very beginning the schools of Utah have given very wholesome and noteworthy attention to matters of character education and good citizenship. The important democratic principle of separation of church and state, recognized in the constitution and in the statutes, does not preclude the teaching of principles and ideals of morality and desirable citizenship in a democracy, and more important, it does not preclude the guiding of individual and group behavior in line with the fundamental virtues and the moral concepts and practices involved in the good life. Teachers both past and present are to be commended for their conscientious attention to such matters.[19a]

State School Office bulletins and outlines for use in relation to character education have received high acclaim by recognized authorities in this field nationally. Early in the history of the state, very noteworthy guides in this field were provided under the authorship of Dr. Milton Bennion.[20]

---

19. Council of State Governments: The Forty-Eight State School Systems, 1949, p. 192.

19a. Regrettable recent statements to the contrary by a governmental official in high office in this state are obviously the result of gross misinformation or biased conclusions based upon the selfish desire to influence legislation in a manner hurtful to education in this state and to the financial advantage of certain groups.

20. Character Education Committee, Milton Benion, chairman. Character Education Supplement to the Utah State Course of Study in Elementary and High Schools. 1929 Revision of 1925 Edition.

Backed by legislative enactment giving further emphasis to the needs in this field, an additional director was appointed to the State School Office Staff in 1940 under the title of "Director of School-Community Relations.[21] Emphasis was placed on the following eight point program, backed by a State Council on School-Community Relations composed of wide representation from various organizations throughout the state:

EIGHT POINTS OF EMPHASIS IN CHARACTER EDUCATION AND SCHOOL-COMMUNITY RELATIONS

1. Emphasis upon the fact that all teachers are character education teachers, that character education is an inherent part of all living and learning; a functioning awareness on the part of all teachers regarding character education possibilities in all relations with students in and out of the classroom, and in all relations among students themselves, and with other people.

2. Stimulation of greater enlightenment regarding scientific facts pertaining to alcohol and narcotics and the development of desirable social attitudes regarding alcohol and narcotics.

3. Recognition of phases of responsibility in relation to certain types of school work such as social studies, health, physical education and recreation, homemaking, etc.

4. Increased and improved emphasis upon organization and administration of effective guidance for all students.

   a. Individual

   b. Group—clubs, special interest organizations, etc.

---

21. The writer was appointed as the first such full-time director for the year 1940-41 while on leave of absence from Brigham Young University.

5. An increased but sane community consciousness regarding character education and youth problems, and more thorough recognition of all influences affecting growth and development of young people.

6. Effective coordination of the efforts of all community groups and organizations interested in and affecting the welfare of youth, such as the school, P. T. A., federated women's clubs, service clubs, civic organizations, chambers of commerce, churches, youth organizations, etc. Organize and keep functioning community coordinating councils for the improvement of the local environment and most effective use of all educative resources and influences, all agencies including youth itself to be represented.

7. Law enforcement for those minorities who do not respond to more positive approaches and who provide detrimental influences for youth.

8. Cooperation with teacher education institutions in further stimulating the application of a functioning philosophy of character education.[22]

Balanced Growing   It is important that all aspects of education receive adequate attention in order to provide desirable integration which necessarily takes place within the individual and groups of individuals in society through the educative process. The writer defines integration as balanced growing, physically, intellectually, socially, emotionally, and spiritually.

Safeguards Against Sectarian or Partisan Control   Sections 12 and 13 of the Constitution were designed to safeguard the public schools against control by organized religious groups or by partisan politics:[23]

"Sec. 12, (No religious or partison tests in schools). Neither religious nor partisan test or qualification

22. Biennial Report of the State Superintendent of Public Instruction, 1941 223 State Capitol, Salt Lake City, Utah.
23. Utah Code Annotated, 1943, Vol. 1, p. 148.

shall be required of any person, as a condition of admission, as teacher or student, into any public educational institution of the state."

Sec. 12 (Public aid to church schools forbidden). Neither the legislature nor any county, city, town, school district or other public corporation, shall make any appropriation to aid in the support of any school, seminary, academy, college, university or other institution controlled in whole, or in part, by any church, sect or denomination whatever."

Vocaltional Education   Vocational education beyond that included in general education in the schools of Utah is carried on principally on the post high school level[24] at two state vocational schools and at the state colleges. The Central Utah Vocational School at Provo and the Salt Lake Area Vocational Sihool at Salt Lake City are operated under the control and direction of the State Board of Education which is designated also as the State Board for Vocational Education with the State Superintendent of Public Instruction as its chief executive officer. These vocational schools are financed by legislative appropriation and student fees. The subject of federal funds for vocational education is included in Chapter X, the Federal Government and Education.

State and Private Colleges and Universities   As might be expected from a people with a long established interest in education, abundant opportunities have been provided for higher education in state and private colleges and universities.[25]

The state system of higher institutions includes the University of Utah, Salt Lake City, Utah; Utah State

---

24. There are programs of vocational education in the high schools, but these programs are essentially part of the large program of general education.

25. Utah has a significantly larger percentage of its population enrolled in colleges and universities than has any other state, and is double the national average in this respect. (Survey by Dean C. E. Partch, School of Education, Rutgers University and printed in Salt Lake Tribune, February 27, 1946)

Agricultural College, Logan; Branch Utah State Agricultural College, Cedar City; Snow Branch Agricultural College, Ephraim; Weber College, Ogden; Dixie College, St. George; and Carbon College at Price. The last three named make up the system of state junior colleges under the State Board of Education. Snow College was also part of the state junior college system from 1932 to 1951 when, by legislative enactment, its status was changed and it became a branch of the Utah State Agricultural College.[26]

The private university and colleges as listed by the State Department of Public Instruction[27] are Brigham Young University, Provo; St. Mary of the Wasatch, Salt Lake City; and Westminster College, Salt Lake City.

Private Schools   Other private schools listed in the directory are Academy St. Mary of the Wasatch, Salt Lake City; St. Ann's School, Salt Lake City; St. Joseph, Ogden; Judge Memorial High School, Salt Lake City; Catholic Schools, Salt Lake City; Rowland Hall, Salt Lake City; Wasatch-Logan Academy, Mt. Pleasant; St. John's Lutheran School, Salt Lake City; McCune School of Music and Art, Salt Lake City; L. D. S. Business College, Salt Lake City; Henager School of Business, Salt Lake City; Ogden Business College, Ogden.

Special Schools and State Agencies   The Intermountain Indian School supported by the federal government is located at Brigham City, Utah.
Americanization schools are maintained in certain sections as provided by law.[28]

Special state institutions established to meet the specific needs of certain atypical groups include the State Industrial School, Ogden; State Training School, American Fork; Utah Schools for the Deaf and the Blind, Ogden; and the Utah Commission for the Blind, Salt Lake City.

---

26. Weber, Snow, and Dixie Colleges were maintained by the L.D.S. Church prior to the time they were made state colleges in 1931 and 1932.
27. Utah Public School Directory, 1950-51.
28. See School Laws of the State of Utah, 1949. pp. 64, 65, and 66.

Certain state agencies, although not strictly part of the educational system of the state, carry on activities which directly or indirectly have a bearing on education. Some of these agencies and organizations are the State Board of Health, The State Historical Society, The Utah State Fair Association, and the Utah State Institute of Fine Arts. The reader may think of others that should be here listed.

This chapter could with profit be supplemented with a great array of statistics and other information regarding classification and numbers of pupils enrolled, attendance, expenditures, programs of instruction, etc. For such information in convenient form, the reader is referred to the Utah School Report.[29]

REFERENCES

Bancroft: History of Utah.

Bennion, Milton: Character Educ. Supplement to the Utah State Course of Study for Elementary and High Schools. Revised Edition, 1929.

Council of State Governments: The Forty-Eight State School Systems, Chicago, Illinois, 1949.

Cowles, LeRoy E.: Organization and Administration of Public Education in Utah, Extension Division, University of Utah, 1949.

Educational Policies Commission, N.E.A.: Moral and Spiritual Values in the Public Schools, 1951. National Education Association, 1201 Sixteenth Street, N.W., Washington, D. C.

Deseret News Editorial, October 15, 1944.

Hughes and Launcelot: Education-America's Magic, Iowa State College Press, Ames, Iowa, 1946.

---

29. Utah School Report is published biennially by the State Superintendent of Public Instruction.

Moffitt, J. C.: The History of Public Education in Utah, 1946.

Moffitt, J. C.: John Rocky Park in Utah's Frontier Culture, 1947.

Salt Lake Tribune, February 27, 1946.

State Superintendent of Public Instruction: Utah School Report, 1948-50 (Also other issues published biennially).

Survey of Education in Utah, 1926, Bulletin No. 18, Bureau of Education, Department of the Interior. U. S. Government Printing Office.

Utah Code Annotated, 1943 and subsequent Session Laws.

Utah State Department of Public Instruction: School Laws of the State of Utah, 1951.

Utah State Department of Public Instruction: Utah Public School Directory.

CHAPTER IV

THE STATE DEPARTMENT OF PUBLIC INSTRUCTION

State Board of Education As indicated in the preceding chapter the constitution of the State of Utah and subsequent legislation provides that the "general control and supervision of the public school system is vested in the state board of education" which is empowered to employ needed personnel and to make and enforce necessary rules and regulations for the carrying out of this responsibility.[1] Duties and functions of the State Board of Education include the following: (a) determination of educational policies; (b) adoption of rules and regulations which have the effect of law; (c) prescription of minimum standards in specific areas; (d) determination of regulations governing the apportionment of state school funds; (e) regulation of teacher certification; (f) appointment of a state course of study committee and state textbook commission; and (g) determination of the plan of organization for the State Department of Education. Also, in addition to these over-all functions, the board is the responsible governing body for the administration of the state junior colleges, adult education, education for the adult blind, and the schools for the deaf and blind. Also, this board has been designated by statute as the State Board for Vocational Education in relation to the provisions of the federal Smith-Hughes Act and related federally aided vocational education.[2]

---

1. School Laws of the State of Utah, 1951. **Article X, Sec. 8, p. 7, and 75-7-7, p. 13.**
2. National Commission for the Defense of Democracy through Education, Harold Benjamin, Chairman, et. al: An Inquiry into the Organization and Administration of the State Education Agency of Utah. 1950. p. 8.

Number,
Term of
Office
How
Selected
The law provides for a non-partisan state board of education of nine members, three of whom are elected each two years for terms of six years. The term of office of a regularly elected member begins January first following his election and continues until January first six years later or until his successor is legally elected and qualified.[3]

The regional election districts for this purpose are the same geographically and bear the same numbers as the judicial districts of the state. There are seven judicial districts or regional districts from each of which one member of the state board of education is elected, except that three (two extra) members are elected from the populous region number three.

The elections are held during the even numbered years as follows: In 1952 and every six years thereafter three members are elected from regional district number 3. In 1954 and every six years thereafter one member is elected from each of regional districts No. 4, 6, and 1. In 1956 and every six years thereafter one member is elected from each of regional districts No. 5, 2, and 7.[4]

Nomination
and Election
of Members
of State
Board of
Education
For each of the above regional districts, on the first Wednesday of March in the years above indicated, the Secretary of State is directed by law to call a regional convention, fixing "the hour and place of said conventions, which shall be not less than thirty days nor more than ninety days from the time said convention is called. He shall appoint a temporary chairman for each convention and at the conclusion of each convention shall certify the name of each and every candidate for the State Board of Education as may be nominated at said convention."

---

3. School Laws of the State of Utah. 1951. 57-7-1. p. 11.
4. Ibid., 75-7-1.10, p. 11 and 75-7-1.50, p. 12.

Each regional district convention shall nominate at least two candidates for each membership in the State Board of Education to which the particular regional school district is entitled as hereinafter specified. In making such nominations the convention shall give consideration only to the merits and fitness and such nomination shall be made irrespective of occupation, party affiliation, religion or sex.

On or before the last Wednesday of September of the year in which a member or members of the state board of education are to be elected as hereinafter provided, any qualified person residing in the district from which a member or members of the state board of education are to be elected, may be nominated for election as a member of the state board of education upon filing with the Secretary of State a petition of nomination signed by not less than fifty qualified and registered electors residing within said election district. On or before October 15th following the receipt of such petition or petitions the Secretary of State shall certify to the clerk of each school district within said election district the name of the person or persons who have qualified for nomination for election to the state board of education. The Secretary of State shall have printed a sufficient number of ballots for election of a member or members to the state board of education, listing the names of candidates with last names in alphabetical order. On or before the last Wednesday of October the Secretary of State shall deliver to the clerk of each school district concerned the number of official ballots requested by said clerk.

There shall be elected on the first Tuesday after the first Monday of November in each election district in which a term of office has expired, one or more members of the state board of education as hereinafter provided. The elections shall be conducted as a part of the general election with the same judges of election, the same constables, and the same polling places, but with separate ballots. Within five days following the election, each district board of education shall canvass the returns of said election in the same manner as provided for canvassing returns of the election of a member of the district board of education. Immediately following such canvass, and in any event not later than November 20th, the clerk of each board of education shall certify to the Secretary of State and to the state board of education the number of votes cast within that school district for each person nominated for election as a member, or members, of the state board of education.

The state board of education, at a meeting attended by the Secretary of State, shall canvass the certified returns of the election not later than December 15th, and the Secretary of State shall immediately issue a certificate of election to the person, or persons, receiving the highest number of votes for the office, or offices, to be filled. A copy of each certificate shall be filed with the secretary of the board of education. The member or members elected shall serve for a term of six years, beginning January 1st following their election, or until their successors are duly elected and qualified.[5]

The reader will note from the above extensive quotation from the 1951 statutes that, although the names of those nominated for possible membership on the state board of education are listed on a separate, non-partisan ballot and the results are canvassed by local boards of

---

5. **Ibid.,** 75-7-1.20, 75-7-1.30, 75-7-1.40, pp. 11 and 13.

eduction and the state board of education, the election is nevertheless held in conjunction with the regular political election in November when many electors are deeply stirred with political considerations. It appears to the writer that it would be highly desirable to institute at some appropriate time a modification in the law which would provide for the election of members of the state board of education on the first Wednesday in December, the time specified for electing members of local boards of education in a completely non-partisan election.

Chairman and Vice-chairman The state board of education, at the first meeting in February of each year, elects from its members a chairman and a vice-chairman who serve as presiding officers of the board.

Appointment of State Superintendent The board is required by law to appoint a professionally qualified state superintendent of public instruction who is the executive officer of the board and whose term of office continues at the pleasure of the board. The salary of the state superintendent is determined by the state board of education.

Secretary The law provides that "the board shall also appoint a secretary of the board who shall serve at the pleasure of the board."[6]

Assistants and Staff Upon the recommendation of the state superintendent, the board appoints "such assistant superintendents, directors, supervisors, assistants, clerical workers, and other employees, as in the judgment of the board may be necessary to the proper administration and supervision of the public school system."[7] The salaries of such employees are determined by the board of education and are paid from funds appropriated for that purpose. For a listing of the state

6. Ibid., 75-7-2, p. 12.
7. Ibid., 75-7-2, p. 12.

school office staff thus appointed the reader should refer to the most recent directory.[8]

Compensation and Expense of Board Members   The members of the state board of education receive an allowance of $300.00 per year plus necessary traveling expenses. The board meets at the call of the chairman and is required by law to meet at least eleven times each year. The position of board member is an important non-salaried position of public service. The small allowance is intended merely as reimbursement or partial reimbursement for loss of time from one's business or employment while attending board meetings.

Filling of Unexpired Terms   When an unexpired term is left through a vacancy caused by a board member's death, resignation, moving from the election district, or other cause, the vacancy is "filled by appointment for the unexpired term by a convention of district school board members called for that purpose."[9] Such convention of local board members within a state board of education election district is called by the chairman of the state board of education or other authorized representative of the board.

Duties of State Superintendent and Staff   With the aid of his staff, and under the direction of the board, the superintendent, as the chief executive officer of the board, is charged with the administration of the system of public instruction and with the general supervision of the schools of the state, and is directed to perform such other duties as the state board of education may require.

The superintendent is required by law to prepare and transmit to the proper officials of school districts "suitable forms and regulations for making all reports, with the necessary blanks therefor, school registers, and necessary

8. Utah State Department of Public Instruction: Utah Public School Directory. 223 State Capitol, Salt Lake City (Latest Edition)
9. School Laws of the State of Utah, 1951, 75-7-1.60, p. 12.

instructions for the organization and government of district schools and conduct of all necessary proceedings."[10]
. . . He has full power to investigate all matters pertaining to the public schools.

The state superintendent certifies to the State Tax Commission and to the state auditor the number of classroom units in each district and the appropriations from state school funds to which each district is entitled under the law. He may examine the state auditor's books and records relative to school revenue and those of other public officials relating to school accounts.

He is directed to visit at least once a year in each county in the state the principal schools and district school boards, to advise with superintendents, school boards, and other school officers upon all matters involving the welfare of the schools. He is further directed to advise with teachers and lecture to institutes and public assemblies upon topics calculated to promote the interests of education.

All school construction plans involving an expenditure of more than $5000.00 in county school districts are subject to the approval of the state superintendent. The state superintendent may call annually a convention of the district and city superintendents, and state law declares it to be the duty of all district and city superintendents to attend such conventions when called.[11]

The state superintendent "shall when requested by superintendents or other school officers give them written answers to all questions concerning the school law. His decisions shall be held to be correct and final until set aside by a court of competent jurisdiction or by subsequent legislation."[12]

The superintendent is required to issue a biennial report of the administration of the system of public in-

10. Ibid., 75-8-3, p. 16.
11. Ibid., 75-8-10, p. 17.
12. Ibid., 75-8-4, p. 16.

struction. He is also directed to furnish the United States Commissioner of Education such information as that officer may require.

The legislature has specified that "the state superintendent, with the approval of the state board of education, shall prepare and submit to the governor to be included in his budget to be submitted to the legislature, a budget of the requirements of his office, including the expenses of the state board of education, for his own and other salaries and wages, office and travel expense, equipment and repairs necessary for carrying out the duties imposed upon the superintendent of public instruction and the state board of education in the administration and supervision of the public school system for the biennium next following the convening of the legislature."[13]

Teaching certificates and other certificates for professional school personnel are granted by the state board of education upon the recommendation of the college of education, school of education, or department of education of the institution in which each respective candidate completes the necessary requirements. These certificates are issued through the office of the director of teacher personnel and the state certification committee appointed by the state board of education upon the recommendation of the state superintendent.

In setting standards and requirements for various types of certification periodically over the years the state board of education receives and considers recommendations democratically arrived at through a sizeable number of representatives of the membership of the organized profession, which recommendations reach the board through its executive officer, the state superintendent.

The five district superintendents who serve as the curriculum committee and textbook commission are ap-

13. Ibid., 75-8-7, p. 17.

pointed by the state board upon the recommendation of the state superintendent.

The state board of education, operating through its executive officer, the superintendent, and his staff, exercises supervision over public libraries as well as school libraries, and is charged by law to "promote the establishment of libraries."[14]

Other duties of the state superintendent as the executive officer of the board with the help of the state school office staff may be recognized by the reader through referring again to the classification of duties and functions of the state board of education given at the beginning of this chapter.

Board Responsible Directly to the People Previously mentioned provisions of constitutional and statute law have long given evidence of the obvious intention of the people to have state and local school systems operated under the control and direction of non-partisan boards, responsible directly to the people and free from control or interference by politically elected public executives selected for other responsibilities of government. This is definitely in line with a fundamental American principle emphasizing the necessity of keeping the schools free from partisan or sectarian denominational controls.

The following is quoted from a recent report by the National Commission for the Defense of Democracy through Education:[15]

"The governor has little, if any, direct legal control over the superintendent or the board of education. While he may remove any member of the board "for immorality, malfeasance in office, incompe-

14. **Ibid.**, 75-7-9, p. 13.
15. National Commission for the Defense of Democracy through Education: An Inquiry into the Organization and Administration of the State Education Agency of Utah, 1950, p. 9. 1201 Sixteenth Street, N.W. Washington 6, D.C.

tency, or continued neglect of duty," this power
has never been invoked.

"The governor has the right to investigate any
state department and make recommendations to
the legislature concerning the work of the department. He has no authority to order. . . . the superintendent of schools to make departmental alter-
ations or changes. . ."

As indicated through constitutional amendments and
legislative enactments the state board of education appoints the state superintendent who is responsible directly
to the board which in turn is elected by and is responsible
directly to the people of the state on a strictly non-partisan
basis. It is expected that the legislature will wisely continue to reflect the will of the people in preserving this
fundamentally American relationship regarding the control of schools.

BIBLIOGRAPHY

Council of State Governments: The Forty-Eight State
School Systems. Chicago, 1949.

National Commission for the Defense of Democracy
through Education, N.E.A.: An Inquiry into the Organization and Administration of the State Education Agency of Utah. 1201 Sixteenth Street, N.W.,
Washington 6, D. C. 1950.

State Department of Public Instruction: School Laws of
the State of Utah. 223 State Capitol, Salt Lake City
(Current Edition).

U. S. Office of Education: State Boards of Education and
Chief State School Officers, Their Status and Legal
Powers. Bulletin 1950, No. 12. U. S. Govt. Printing
Office, Washington, D. C.

U. S. Office of Education: The Function of State Departments of Education. Misc. No. 12. U. S. Government Printing Office, Washington, D. C.

CHAPTER V

THE ORGANIZATION AND ADMINISTRATION
OF THE SCHOOL DISTRICT

*Arm of
the State*
As explained in Chapter III, Utah's forty school districts[1] were created by legislative enactment based on constitutional mandate and authority. These school districts are arms of the state and are not local subdivisions of city and county governments. District boards of education and their appointed officials derive their authority from state law. City and county governments as such do not have supervision and control of the local school districts. The district board of education is responsible directly to the people of the district and to the people of the entire state through the elected, non-partisan state board of education described in Chapter IV.

State school law does, however, give boards of county commissioners two duties as a service to school districts, one of which occurs annually and the other occasionally: (1) When the board of education has according to its legal rights and powers adopted the school budget for the ensuing year and has determined the tax levy necessary to raise funds for such budget, having reported the same to the board of county commissioners, the commission is then obligated under the law to levy the tax sufficient to raise said funds. Within the limits of state law, the discretionary power in the matter is with the board of education. (2) The representative precincts from which members of boards of education are elected sometimes get out of proportion in relative size and the county commissioners are empowered once each five years (October 1936, 1941, 1946, 1951, etc.) to readjust the boundaries of these

---

1. Five city school districts in cities of the first and second class and thirty-five consolidated districts.

precincts of the school district or districts within the county.[2] The reader should note that this is the case as applied to school representative precincts within a district, but not as between school districts. "County commissioners have no right to change existing boundary lines of county school districts. This may be done either by legislative enactment or as provided in Section 75-9-2." [3 and 4]

Most of the consolidated school districts comprise the entire area of the county, but in a few counties as explained in Chapter III there is more than one school district. Outside the first and second class cities there are two school districts in each of Salt Lake, Utah, Juab, and Sanpete counties. There are three school districts in Summit County. Section 75-9-1[5] provides a means whereby these districts within a county, and outside of cities of the first and second class, can be consolidated into one school district by petition and vote of the people if and when they desire to do so. Such a procedure has not occurred since the compulsory consolidation law of 1915 resulted in the present forty school districts, but below is a quotation indicating the manner in which it might be done: This could reduce the number of districts by only six, however.

When there shall be presented to a board of county commissioners a petition signed by twenty per cent of the qualified electors in each of the two or more county school districts, praying for the submission of the question of uniting said districts into a county school district, the board of county commissioners shall submit the question of consolidating such districts into a county school district at the next general election to the qualified electors of such districts. . . Before consolidation shall be established, the vote for consolidation shall be equal

2. School Laws of the State of Utah, 1949. 75-9-3. p. 38.
3. Ibid., Ruling of Attorney General No. 51, p. 100.
4. Ibid., p. 38.

to, or greater than, a majority of the number of votes cast for congressman in each of the districts affected.[5]

The law provides that each city of the first and second class shall constitute one school district, and that the public school system in these cities shall be controlled by the board of education of such cities separate and apart from the counties in which the cities are located.[6] As already indicated, the city school district, as well as the county school district, is an arm of the state.

Board of Education   The board of education of each of the thirty-five county school districts, often referred to as consolidated school districts, consists of five members, one from each of the five precincts. One member is elected each year for a term of five years. The four school districts that are in cities of the second class[7] also each have a board of education of five members, one elected from and by each municipal ward with one member being elected each year for a term of five years.[8]

The board of education of the Salt Lake City School District, in a city of the first class ,consists of twelve members, two from each of six municipal wards. There is elected each even numbered year one member from each municipal ward for a term of four years.[9] In the judgment of the writer it would be highly advantageous in terms of desirable school organization and administration to change the law so as to provide this district with a board of education of five members, one elected each year for a term of five years, the same as in the other districts.

---

5. Ibid., p. 38.
6. Ibid., 75-9-4 and 5, p. 38.
7. Ogden, Provo, Logan, and Murray.
8. Schol Laws of the State of Utah, 1949. 75-9-6 and 75-10-3, pp. 38 and 40.
9. Ibid., 75-9-6 and 75-10-2, pp. 38 and 40.

*Election
of Board
Members*
In all school districts of the state, members of boards of education are elected at non-partisan elections held on the first Wednesday in December entirely separate from the regular political election which is held early in November. The board of education provides at least one voting place in each precinct or municipal ward from which a member is to be elected, appoints the judges of election, furnishes the official ballots, receives the reports of the judges, officially canvases the results at a meeting of the board, and author-izes the payment from school funds of all lawful and necessary expenses of the election.

The law requires the county clerk to furnish free of charge to the board of education at least five days previous to the day of such election a certified copy of the registra-tion list showing the names of all qualified electors resid-ing in the election districts within the school district.

Each candidate for election or reelection, or at least five citizens in his behalf, must file with the clerk of the board of education not less than fifteen days next preced ing the day of election a signed statement announcing that he or she is a candidate. The names of those for whom notices of candidacy are received by the clerk within the designated time limit are made public and are placed on the official printed ballots. However, voters may legally write in the names of others not printed on the ballots if they wish to do so. No provision is made for absentee ballots.[10]

*Qualifica-
tions of
Board
Members*
A member of the board of education is required to be and to remain a resident and a qualified and registered elector in the rep-resentative precinct or municipal ward from which he is selected in order to be eligible for the position.[11] State law specifies no other qualifica-tions. Apparently the legislature preferred to trust the

10. **Ibid.,** Chapters 9 and 10, **pp. 38-40.**
11. **Ibid.,** 75-10-4, p. 40.

people to use their good judgment in electing high calibre persons to this important position. Members of boards of education before entering upon the discharge of their duties must qualify by taking and subscribing to the constitutional oath of office. They are required to thus qualify before taking their seats at the first regular meeting in January next after their election, and they serve until their successors are duly elected and qualified.[12]

According to state law and the opinions of the attorney general, a board member cannot at the same time be the superintendent, a principal or a teacher or be financially involved in any contract or business transaction with the school district. A person cannot at the same time be a member of the legislature and a member of a board of education, but he can, if elected, be a board member and a county commissioner. A teacher, however, may if elected or appointed be a member of the legislature.[13]

Filling of Unexpired Terms In case of a vacancy leaving an unexpired term because of death, resignation, or disqualifying of a board member, the vacancy is filled through appointment by the board of education. The person appointed must be a resident and qualified elector in the school precinct or ward from which the former member was elected. The appointment is for the unexpired term except that in Salt Lake City the appointee is to serve until the next school board election in the city. As a means of preventing delay, the law requires a city board of education to fill such a school board vacancy within thirty days, and if it fails to do so the city commission makes the appointment. No such time limit has been written into the law for consolidated, county school districts.[14]

12. **Ibid.**, 75-11-1 and 2, p. 41.
13. **Ibid.**, Attorney General's Opinions 25-32, p. 98 and 99.
14. **Ibid.**, 75-10-4. Opinions of Attorney General 46 and 47, p. 100.

Organization of Board
Members of the board of education organize by electing from their number a president and a vice president whose term of office is two years and until their successors are elected and qualified, but the attorney general has ruled that a board of education if it cares to do so may adopt a policy of electing a president and a vice president annually.[15] The organization meeting is the first regular meeting of the board of education in January.

It is mandatory for the board of education to appoint a superintendent of schools who is the chief executive officer of the board, a clerk, and a treasurer, each of whose term of office is two years, and it may appoint such other officers that in its judgment may be necessary. The term of office of the superintendent starts July 1 with the beginning of the fiscal year while the terms of office of the clerk and treasurer begin in January.[16]

Compensation and Expenses
It is intended that board members be selected from among civic minded, public spirited citizens whose principal motive in running for office is public service rather than personal financial gain. The compensation, therefore, is intended only to compensate, or more correctly to partially compensate, for loss of time from a member's employment while attending meetings of the board of education. The law provides for the compensation to be fixed by the board of education, but specifies that such compensation shall be fixed at a sum not to exceed $100 each per year in city school districts and not to exceed $150 each per year in county school districts and traveling expenses not to exceed $100 per year, provided, in county school districts any member living more than 75 miles from the place of meeting may receive not to exceed $200 per year for traveling expenses. Each member is required to submit an itemized account of traveling expenses sworn to by him

15. Ibid., 75-11-3, p. 41, and Opinion of Attorney General No. 13, p. 98.
16. Ibid., 75-11-3 and 75-11-11, p. 41.

and approved by the board. This is principally for travel to and from board meetings. The superintendent and assistants are normally expected to do the traveling necessary in connection with carrying out the policies and decisions of the board.[17]

Body
Corporate
The board of education is a body corporate which may sue and be sued, and may take, hold, lease, sell, and convey real and personal property as the interests of the schools may require.[18] The board is empowered by law to "do all things needful for the maintenance, prosperity and success of the schools, and the promotion of education; and may adopt by-laws and rules for its own procedure, and make and enforce all needful rules and regulations for the control and management of the public schools of the district."[19] For an example of such a set of published rules and regulations of a board of education the reader is referred to the office of one of the school districts.[20]

Committee
of the
Whole
It is highly desirable that the board as a school district legislating, policy making, decision making body (with employed executives to carry out its decisions), should act in practically all matters as a committee of the whole with professional advisement and recommendations from its employed chief executive, the superintendent, rather than divide itself into a number of permanent standing committees each doing part of the work of the board and sometimes, under a misimpression of function, actually doing part of the work intended to be done by its employed officers. When committees are used they should be appointed by the president in fulfillment of a decision of the board as special, temporary committees to be dis-

---

17. **Ibid.**, 75-11-8, p. 41.
18. **Ibid.**, 75-9-8, p. 38.
19. **Ibid.**, 75-11-20 and 21, p. 43 and Opinions of Attorney General Nos. 52-58, pp. 100 and 101.
20. Most Utah school districts will have a handbook of printed rules and regulations.

solved when their special, limited assignments are completed.

Joint Rather Than Individual Authority It is the function of members of the board of education to jointly use sound judgment in the making of policies and decisions in relation to the schools. Outside of board meetings members of the board have no individual authority except as it is specially delegated by the board for a particular purpose at a given time. Valid, legally binding decisions of the board, including the authorization of expenditures, can be made only at board meetings by a majority vote of the membership of the board, and board members, including their presiding officers, are not expected to individually spend time between meetings doing work for which their executives and staff assistants are employed. They will, however, wish to study and think and be well informed so as to render effective and wise judgments when matters of importance are presented and considered at board meetings. It is also an excellent thing for them to attend educational conferences, conventions, and institutes whenever possible. They, as well as all responsible members of the community, are, of course, welcome to visit any of the schools, but they will not individually attempt to supervise the teaching and other services at the school for which purpose the superintendent and his staff are employed by the board. Each board member should feel jointly responsible with the other members and the superintendent for the welfare of all the schools of the entire district and not just for the schools in the area from which he or she was elected.

President and Vice-President The president of the board of education presides at all meetings of the board, appoints committees authorized by the board, and signs all warrants ordered by the board to be drawn upon the treasurer. In case of the absence or disability of the president, his duties are performed by the

vice president.[21] Although called upon by law to perform
the above specifically mentioned duties as presiding officers, the president and vice president have no more individual authority in the making of the decisions of the
board than do any of the other members. They vote regularly on matters which come before the board, and each
of their votes counts exactly the same as the vote of any
other member. As emphasized above, it is the board as a
whole that makes binding decisions through action in
board meetings.

*Superintendent
of Schools*   While the president and vice president are the presiding officers of the
board of education, the superintendent
of schools is the chief executive officer of the board, selected and employed by the board as its professional advisor
to make recommendations to it and, as its executive officer, to carry out or to see that its actions and policies are
executed or carried out. An officer responsible to the
board of education, the superintendent is the general administrative and supervisory head of the school system of
the district. He should attend all regular and special meetings of the board, except perhaps when the board goes into
executive session to consider his own reappointment, and
he is obligated to give his recommendations on matters
considered by the board. In a properly ordered school
system he exercises the right of initiation of policies to be
considered for adoption and the right of nomination of all
school employees of the district who, of course, can be
employed only when approved by the board of education.

The law provides that the superintendent shall act
as the budget officer of the district.[22] With assistance
which he wisely requests from the clerk, the principals,
teachers, and other needed help, the superintendent prepares and submits the annual tentative budget which
should be based on the educational needs of the district

21. School Laws of the State of Utah, 1949. 75-11-14, p. 42.
22. Ibid., 75-21-1, p. 60.

and other necessary factors. The tentative, recommended budget becomes the accepted budget of the district, sometimes with modifications, only when adopted by the board of education in line with procedures which are explained in greater detail in Chapter VII.

The superintendent is required to hold and to keep in force the Administrators Certificate for Superintendents issued under the authority of the state board of education which requires at the present time the master's degree or its equivalent which must include certain specific professional education requirements and at least three years of successful teaching and/or administrative experience. His salary is determined by the board of education.

As the chief executive of the board, the superintendent has supervision of the schools, the supervisors, principals, teachers, engineers, custodians, drivers, and other employees. In some of the larger districts he has the help of one or more assistant superintendents. He, and through him the board, is represented in each school by the principal who is both an administrator and a supervisor in his school. As a wise and democratic administrator he will frequently make use of committees of teachers in the solution of administrative, supervisory, and curricular problems of the district.

The superintendent makes an annual written report to the board of education at or before the first regular meeting in August.[23]

Supervisors Although some superintendents still prefer to have their general and special elementary and secondary school supervisors carry administrative responsibility, many prefer otherwise. A predominance of the specialists in educational supervision prefer to have these supervisors unencumbered with line administrative authority so they can be free to use only the authority of expertness and genuine helpfulness as they

---

23. Ibid., 75-11-17, p. 42.

work helpfully with teachers, principals and others while recognizing that the principal is administratively in charge of his school. It is also very noticeable that teachers and principals are relatively much freer to seek supervisory help under this plan.

Supervisors and principals must hold the Administrative-Supervisory Certificate for the division of the school system (either elementary or secondary) in which they work.

Clerk and Treasurer   The clerk and treasurer are appointed by the board for terms of two years and until their successors are appointed and qualified. The clerk and treasurer may be two separate persons or, at the discretion of the board, the same person may hold both positions.[24]

Before entering upon the discharge of their duties the clerk and the treasurer are each required to give a bond to the board of education in such sum and in such manner as prescribed and approved by the board, and are also required to take and subscribe to the constitutional oath of office.

It is the duty of the clerk to attend all meetings of the board; to keep an accurate journal of its proceedings, and have the care and custody of the seal, records, and legal papers; to countersign all warrants drawn upon the treasurer by order of the board; to keep an accurate account of all moneys received and paid out; and to prepare and submit to the board an annual financial statement under oath, of the receipts and disbursements during the fiscal year ending June 30, which statement the board is required by law to have published in a newspaper having general circulation in the district.[25]

The clerk prepares and submits the "Annual Financial Report" to the state superintendent, and either pre-

24. Ibid., 75-11-3, p. 41.
25. Ibid., 75-11-15, p. 42 and Opinions of the Attorney General Nos. 147-151, p. 107.

pares or materially assists the superintendent in preparing the "Annual Statistical Report" to the state superintendent and such other reports as the superintendent and board may require.

He checks and complies the reports of the school census enumerators and forwards an official report of the school census to the state superintendent as required by law.[26]

Each month at or prior to the regular meeting, the clerk furnishes to the superintendent and to each member of the board of education a report setting forth the amounts of all budget appropriations, the disbursements to date for such appropriations, and the amounts remaining. Such reports are provided to the superintendent whenever needed for study and planning in relation to the administration of the school district and particularly the budget.

Upon the recommendation of the superintendent who is in close touch with the instructional programs and educational needs, such recommendation usually being given in the form of an O.K. placed on the requisitions submitted by the principals, the clerk orders the books, supplies, materials and equipment for the various schools and sees that they are properly distributed.

He carries on such official correspondence as may be necessary, keeps such records, and performs such other duties as may be required.

The treasurer is the custodian of all moneys belonging to the corporation (school district) and is responsible upon his bond for all moneys received by him as treasurer. He prepares and submits in writing a monthly report (sometimes more often) of the receipts and disbursements of his office, and pays out moneys only upon a warrant signed by the president, or in his absence by the vice president, and countersigned by the clerk. The law pro-

---

26. **Ibid.**, 75-11-12 and 13.

vides that "he shall perform such other duties as the board may require."[27]

Audit   The law requires the board to have a recognized, licensed public accountant make at least biennially an official financial audit of the books of the district. This audit should cover moneys handled by employees and all organizations at individual schools as well as the books of the clerk and treasurer.

Principal   As already indicated, the principal is the representative of the superintendent at the individual school. He also represents the teachers, pupils, and patrons of his school to the superintendent and through him to the board. Administratively speaking, although it is recognized that he should be a democratic leader in the full sense of the term, the principal has general supervision and control of his school, including pupils, teachers, custodians, drivers, and other workers. He is in charge of the building, grounds, and school property and should see that they are kept in good condition. The discipline of the school is necessarily a cooperative affair in relation to the education of the pupils.[28]

The principal is expected to make reports and recommendations to the superintendent regarding the teachers and other employees of the school. With the cooperation of his staff he keeps records, inventories, makes reports, requisitions, payrolls, etc. It is highly important he and his staff participate cooperatively in providing data and recommendations pertaining to the budget.

Teachers and Pupils   The major purpose of all the foregoing organizational, administrative, and supervisory functions treated in this volume is to provide the kinds of situations and conditions in which the best kind of teaching and learning can take place. Without the important work of the teachers it

27. **Ibid.,** 75-11-16, p. 42.
28. **See** Chapter VI.

would all be in vain. The teachers and pupils do not exist for the organization, but the organization exists to enhance teaching through providing system, orderly procedure, security, stability, and challenging opportunity. With this in mind the reader may wish to refer to Chart I for a simplified diagram of organizational and administrative relationships.

Teachers are required to hold valid teaching certificates for the level at which they teach. The specific requirements differ as between elementary and secondary certification, but the minimum number of years of college preparation required at either level is four years terminating in the bachelor's degree or its equivalent. The secondary certificate for junior and senior high schools (grades 7 to 12) does not carry the right to teach in the elementary schools (kdg. to 6th) and visa versa. The requirements for these certificates may be found in the annual catalogues of the senior colleges and universities in the state. By taking sufficient extra preparation both certificates may be obtained if desired, but it is recommended that ample preparation be first obtained for one or the other. There are, of course, a number of elements in common between the two sets of requirements.

Liabilities   The law provides that members of a board of education may be held personally liable for any salary payments to uncertified or unauthorized teachers, supervisors, or administrators except for short-term substituting in place of a regular teacher. A board member, school administrator, or teacher is not liable for accidental injuries sustained by pupils at school or while on their way to or from school unless such injury is the result of personal negligence on the part of such board member, school administrator, or teacher.[29]

---

29. School Laws of the State of Utah, 1949. Opinions of the Attorney General Nos. 165 and 166, pp. 108 and 109.

*Display
of Flag*   State law requires the display of the American flag at public schools as follows:

It shall be the duty of every board of education to provide each school house or the grounds thereof with a suitable flagpole and to cause the American flag to be displayed thereon every school day during school hours and during the daylight hours of every national and state holiday and on Flag Day of each year except in case of rain, snow, or high wind, and that the flag shall be maintained in an unfaded and respectable condition at all times; provided, however, that schools having no regular caretaker during the summer months shall not be required to display the flag on holidays which fall during the season when school is not in session.[30]

*Transportation
of Pupils*   There are two principal phases to consolidation. One has to do with the size of school districts as administrative units in which there may be quite a number of schools. The other phase has to do with the transportation of pupils to various centers for better organized, well-equipped schools in place of so many tiny, poorly equipped schools in various locations wherever a few families may have settled. According to U. S. Office of Education reports, Utah has a smaller percentage of its pupils in one teacher schools than any other state, and a large number of pupils are transported in modern school busses. It will be noted in Chapter VII that, as part of the minimum school program, the sum of $675,000 per year has been distributed by the state to school districts to help bear the cost of pupil transportation. It has been recommended to the leg-

---

30. Ibid., 75-24-1, p. 62.

Chart I
Line and Staff Relationships in the School District

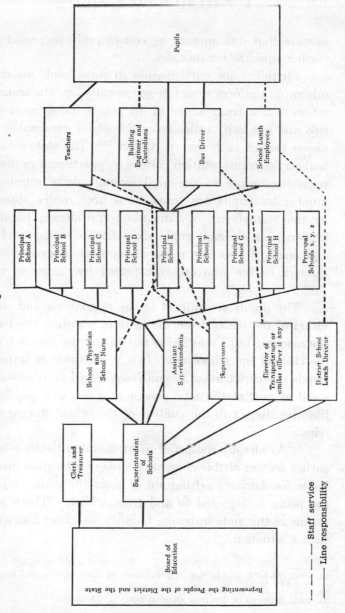

Pupils

Teachers

Building Engineer and Custodians

Bus Driver

School Lunch Employees

Principal School A

Principal School B

Principal School C

Principal School D

Principal School E

Principal School F

Principal School G

Principal School H

Principal Schools x, y, z

School Physician and School Nurse

Assistant Superintendents

Supervisors

Director of Transportation or similar officer if any

District School Lunch Director

Clerk and Treasurer

Superintendent of Schools

Board of Education

Representing the People of the District and the State

- - - - Staff service

———— Line responsibility

islature that this amount be considerably increased as a further equalization measure.

Eligibility for participation in state funds under the minimum uniform school program calls for "the transportation to and from school of all pupils living more than two and one-half miles from school, or reasonable provision toward such transportation."[31] The state's contributions for transportation costs are apportioned to the districts "according to the total average daily number of pupil-miles pupils are transported over routes approved by the State Board of Education, considering pupils in kindergarten through grade six, who are transported one and one-half miles or more and pupils in grades seven through twelve who are transported two miles or more . . ."[32]

The pupils are subject to the regulations and supervision of the school from the time of boarding the bus in the morning until they leave the bus on the return trip at the close of the school day. It is permissible to transport pupils in district buses to and from school activities sponsored as part of the total school program and pupils are likewise subject to the control of the school during such trips.

As already indicated in mentioning liability in an earlier section of this chapter, boards of education are not liable for damages arising out of accidents while children are being transported to and from school. "There is no statute in this state imposing liability on school districts in such a situation."[33]

---

31. **Ibid.**, 75-7-24, p. 14. See also Opinions of Attorney General Nos. 179 and 180, p. 110.
32. **Ibid.**, 75-12-7, pp. 46 and 47.
33. **Ibid.**, Opinions of Attorney General Nos. 71, 73, p. 102.

The insurance law of 1943 does not require boards of education to insure school busses, but they are permitted to insure them if they desire to do so.[34]

Experience over many years, supported by extensive data, shows that it is both more desirable and more economical to operate district owned busses than to contract with bus drivers who own their own busses.

There are many regulations regarding the safe operation of school busses, including the stopping at all railroad crossings, inpection of busses, etc. For an indication of some of these regulations the reader is referred to a set of rules and regulations mentioned earlier in this chapter.

Safety Patrols   School officials, teachers, and parents are sufficiently concerned with the details of the law regarding school safety patrols that it is here quoted verbatum:

In every school district, the board of education shall have power and authority to organize school safety patrols, to adopt regulations covering and permitting the flagging of school busses by a school safety patrol member, of the age of eleven years or over, and, with the written permission of a parent or guardian, to appoint pupils as members thereof, for the purpose of influencing and encouraging the other pupils to refrain from crossing public highways at points other than at regular crossings, of influencing and encouraging pupils to refrain from crossing at regular crossings when the presence of traffic would render such crossing unsafe, and of assisting drivers of school busses in maintaining safety rules and in ascertaining that pupils are received and discharged from such busses in safety. Nothing herein contained shall be construed to authorize or permit the use of any safety patrol member for the purpose of directing vehicular traffic, provided that this shall not prohibit the use of a flag or other approved signal by safety patrol member for the purpose of indicating to the driver that school children are crossing the street, nor shall any safety patrol member be stationed in that portion of the highway intended for the use of vehicular traffic, but shall perform his duties from the curb and sidewalk areas. No liability shall attach either to the school district, the board of education, or any individual member thereof, a superintendent, teacher, safety patrol member, parents of safety patrol member or other school authority by virtue of the organization, maintenance, or operation of a school safety patrol, organized, maintained, and operated under authority of this act, provided that the use of any pupil as a safety patrol without the written permission of a parent or guardian by any teacher or board member shall be a misdemeanor.[35]

Course of Study and Textbooks   It is expected that the staff of school districts will augment the state course of study and will make adaptations, adjustments, and additions in relation to the local situation and the pupils taught. No modern teacher can expect to have everything that is needed handed to him or her ready made in the form to be used, but must expect to use initiative and do considerable planning of his

35. **Ibid.**, 75-14a-1, pp. 52 and 53 or Laws of 1947 Chapter 85, p. 371.

own. County school districts are required by law to select their textbooks from the list officially adopted by the state, but this requirement does not apply to the city school districts.

In most respects the determination of what is to be included in the course of study has been left by the legis-- lature to the state course of study committee, but, among other things, the law has specified the teaching of physiol- ogy and hygiene, sanitation and the prevention of disease, the harmful effects of alcohol, tobacco, and other narcotics, worthy ideals and desirable character habits, observance of Bird Day the last Friday in April, appropriate lessons in relation to legal holidays, and the constitutions of the United States and the state of Utah.[36] The student of edu- cation will give extensive attention to what to teach and how and when to teach to best advantage in relation to courses in curriculum and methods, student teaching, etc.

Libraries   Legal provision is provided for the en- couragement of effort to establish and main- tain good school libraries and for cooperation with county and city library systems.[37] It is highly important for schools and communities to have good libraries, well sup- plied with a variety of appropriate books, magazines, and periodicals. In each school of sufficient size it is well to operate a central library, but such central library should not eliminate classroom libraries for frequent and immedi- ate use in connection with many activities that go on in the rooms. A working relationship should be maintained between classroom libraries and central library so that boxes of books can be borrowed at a time for use in the classroom in addition to the individual student borrowing from the central library. If schools are too small for both a central library and classroom libraries, the preference should go to the classroom libraries. Particularly is this

36. **Ibid.,** Chapter 16, 75-16-1 to 11, pp. 54 and 55.
37. **Ibid.,** 75-7-9, p .12; also 51-2-12, p. 85.

true of very small elementary schools. Both central and classroom libraries should be accessioned, classified, and catalogued according to the simplified Dewey Decimal System to provide for convenient and maximum use.

To be eligible to participate in the funds for the state minimum school program, school districts must each year spend at least a minimum amount per pupil in supplying books, bulletins, magazines, etc. for their school libraries. This minimum amount is set by the State Board of Education. Most districts will wisely and consistently spend considerably more than the minimum each year for this purpose.

Other Items Related to the School District
There are many other important items related to the organization and administration of education in the school district which are treated in other sections of this volume and with which the reader is already familiar or will become familiar. It is suggested that certain areas and problems which, within the purpose of this publication or the space abailable, have not been included, may make excellent topics for individual investigation and report. There is really no entirely logical place to stop in the treatment of a subject such as the one under consideration. We turn next to the organization and management of the individual school.

BIBLIOGRAPHY

Campbell: The Work of the School Board Member. State School Board Association of Utah.

Council of State Governments: The Book of the States, 1950-51. Volume VIII. Chicago, Illinois, 1951.

Davies, Daniel R. and Hasler, Fred W.: The Challenge of School Board Membership. New York, Chartwell House, 1949.

Garber, Lee O.: Yearbook of School Law. 3812 Walnut Street, Philadelphia 4, Pennsylvania, 1950.

Marke, David: Educational Law Simplified. New York, Oceana Publications, 1949.

National Education Association. Committee on School Reorganization: Key to Better Education. 1201 Sixteenth Street, N.W., Washington, D. C. 1947.

National Education Association. Committee on School Reorganization: Your School District. 1201 Sixteenth Street, N.W., Washington, D. C. 1948.

Remmlein, Madaline Kinter: School Law. McGraw-Hill. 1950.

Rules and Regulations of the Board of Education, Duchesne County School District, Duchesne, Utah.

Rules and Regulations of the Board of Education, Granite School District, 1950-51.

Sears, Jess B.: Public School Administration. New York, Ronald Press. 1947.

Utah State Department of Public Instruction, E. Allen Bateman, Superintendent: School Laws of the State of Utah, 1949 (also 1951).

CHAPTER VI

THE ORGANIZATION AND MANAGEMENT
OF THE INDIVIDUAL SCHOOL

Function of
Administration
State and district organization exists to make possible and to enhance the work of the individual school for the benefit of the pupils. The organization and management of the individual school are for the purpose of facilitating to the best possible advantage the teaching-learning situations in which school learning takes place in close touch with home and community life.

Administration is a service to the educative process and should be a highly cooperative affair with the principal serving in the capacity of helpful leadership among a staff of professional teachers and other workers actuated by service motives and skilled in the democratic processes. Larger schools are sometimes permitted to also have the services of a vice principal.

Principal
The name, principal, originated from the practice years ago of designating one of the teachers as principal teacher in situations where the enrollment increased so that one teacher could no longer teach the entire group alone and the assistance of one or more additional teachers was provided for the school.

Types of
Organization
In most districts of the state the elementary schools include kindergarten to and including the sixth grade; the junior high schools include grades seven, eight, and nine; and grades ten, eleven, and twelve are included in the senior high school. This type of classification is known as the kindergarten 6-3-3 plan. In some places the 8-4 plan is used with no junior high school organization. In a few places grades eleven and twelve are included in the same institution with the junior college and the schools are operated under what is called the kindergarten 6-4-4 plan.

Typically, the children and youth of Utah receive their elementary and secondary education in elementary schools, junior high schools, and senior high schools. Ordinarily grades seven through twelve are classed as secondary and kindergarten through sixth as elementary.

You probably remember rather clearly the elementary and secondary schools which you attended. What changes, if any, would you recommend in their organization and management? Why? Keep these proposed improvements in mind, revising them and evaluating them as you move forward with your study of education.

Administrative Relationships   The principal, teachers, custodians, and other employees of each school are employed by the board of education upon the recommendation of the superintendent. The superintendent will usually expect a recommendation from the principal regarding the employment or re-employment of the employees of the school for which he is responsible. While the procedure should be quite democratic throughont as already indicated, and committees will be at work on various problems, legally speaking, the teachers and other employees are responsible directly to the principal, the principal to the superintendent, the superintendent to the board of education, as an orderly and systematic means of enhancing the work of teaching for which the school is operated. The principal, as both an administrator and a supervisor, stands in a position of helpfulness to teachers and pupils. He not only represents the superintendent in his school, but he in turn represents the staff, the pupils and patrons to the superintendent and through him to the board of education.

A Test for the Teacher   Each teacher in carrying on his part of the cooperative endeavor may very well at frequent intervals ask himself the following questions:[1]

---

1. The Journal of Education, "A Test for the Teacher." February, 1947.

1. Do I play fair with my fellow teachers, not criticising them, not chiseling, doing my share of the work and a little more, and helping maintain a hopeful outlook?

2. Do I cooperate loyally with the administration?

3. In the classroom, am I the friendly guide, rather than the dictator and tyrant?

4. By precept and example, do I teach my pupils courtesy and consideration for other people?

5. Do I help my pupils break loose from their prejudices and careless generalizations as to certain groups, races, religions and nations?

6. Do I get my pupils to engage in activities that will aid the community?

7. Do my pupils have a definite share in governing their own conduct and in fixing behavior standards as a class?

8. In my contacts with parents, do I try to learn what I can from them before asserting my views, and do I avoid a know-it-all attitude?

9. Am I on good terms with my neighbors and casual acquaintances?

10. Have I joined actively in one or more local groups working toward higher ideals—religious, intellectual or social?

Extension of Home Life The school should be an extension and not a violation of the best kind of home life. It should be a place of warm friendliness, courteous helpfulness, and understandings based on cooperatively developed standards of behavior and responsibility, with the students sharing extensively in school government. Such a school will be a place of welcome for parents and other members of the community who will frequently be found serving on committees and being helpful in various ways.

Such a school will not lock the pupils out until nine

o'clock and then march them into the building in lock-step, military fashion, but will make them feel welcome to enter the building as they arrive, walk in individaully and in small groups, observing cheerfully the courtesies of young ladies and gentlemen, proceeding to their rooms to greet the teacher and be greeted by him and by other pupils, and then proceed to occupy their time in a manner befitting a classroom full of opportunity. Such an atmosphere increases both the amount and the permanency of desirable learning, and builds emotional health and balance.

School Management Discipline of the school should not be thought of as something separate and apart from the school learning, but rather as an integral part of desirable school learnings which enhance balanced growing. Of course, good school management in which all staff members cooperate helps to prevent the occurrence of disciplinary problems. A school in which each teacher is concerned merely with the behavior of his own class of pupils while they are in his own classroom and in which the pupils otherwise find it convenient to merely dodge from the attention of the principal is a poorly organized and poorly managed school.

The "well disciplined" school and classroom should emphasize full participation in purposeful activity and should avoid both chaotic confusion and autocratic regimentation. Such a program should foster the development of a spirit of cooperative independence, self-respect, respect for the rights of others, and respect for a job well done.

The following set of principles or criteria pertaining to teacher-pupil relations are suggested for thoughtful consideration:

TEACHER-PUPIL RELATIONS

1. The basic principles of teaching and learning apply to conduct (behavior) learnings as well as to co-called academic learnings.

2. Conduct is not as general as we once thought. It is more specific. Conduct learnings come as specific learnings in specific situations, and then these specific learnings tend to become associated into general patterns of conduct. For example, children learn a whole series of honesties in many specific situations and not just honesty in general.

3. Children learn what they live, what they do, and in relation to place, time, persons, and conditions. If they make disturbances, they are learning specifically to make disturbances. It is actually possible to teach more harm than good by the way we let children act. The whole situation tends to become part of the learning.

4. Avoid the common misconceptions of discipline.

   (a) Discipline is not something separate and apart from the learning. Good discipline is inherent in good teaching and learning.

   (b) Modern freedom means opportunity for intelligent self direction, not license.

   (c) Avoid preaching at students about conduct.

5. Keep a jump or so ahead of the situation and prevent discipline problems from arising or becoming acute.

6. Distinguish between the best educative discipline and emergency discipline. When we have to use drastic emergency measures of control we have only momentarily saved the day; the real job still lies ahead.

7. We are drunk in our worship of external rewards and punishments. Help pupils to seek genuine values, to see real issues (cause and effect relationships) and genuine interest; not, "How will teacher reward me?" or "How will he punish me?"

8. Let satisfaction accompany the right and dissatisfaction or annoyance attend the wrong. We too often neglect the first and most important half of this principle.

9. A wholesome sense of humor on the part of the teacher is a saving grace.

10. Avoid sarcasm and insult. They get in the way of good teaching, and are far beneath the true expression of a really great soul.

11. Show a wholesome enthusiasm; really believe in what you are doing.

12. Take an individual interest in students.

13. Consult privately with problem cases.

14. Avoid making too many rules. Cooperatively developed standards are better.

15. Actively recognize individual differences. Do not try to treat every child exactly alike. To do so is really very undemocratic.

16. Be specific in attacking your problems. The whole class is not noisy; individual students are noisy (refer again to number 5).

17. Avoid putting teacher against pupil and pupil against teacher. The inconsiderate pupil is guilty of an offense against the group, not just against the teacher.

18. The still, quiet child isn't always the safe child. Be concerned about the timid, shy child who seldom responds.

19. Be consistent and always expect desirable responses.

20. Avoid letting problems pile up to the breaking point. We can unwittingly make our serious discipline problems.

21. Be positive rather than negative. Positive teaching is much more potent than is negative teaching.

22. Help students to learn to act on thinking rather than on mere impulse. So teach that the students often have the experience of having (a) *shared interest* in the problem, project, or enterprise, (b) an opportunity to help in *planning* the method of attack, (c) active *participation* in seeking the solution or in carrying forward the enterprise, (d) a share in the *evaluating* of procedures and accomplishments. (Adapted from Kilpatrick).

23. Someone has said that strength and struggle travel together, but it is really strength and successful struggle which go together.

24. Be mindful of the need for satisfying the basic social urges among which are: (1) satisfying expression, (2) status, (3) security, and (4) new experience.

25. Three levels of living are : (a) the "have to" level, (b) the "ought to" level, and (c) the "want to" level. Are you moving your students from the "have to" toward the "want to" level?

26. Wherever and whenever possible make use of helpful cooperation rather than competition except, perhaps, in friendly play.

27. Make intelligent use of cause and effect relationships. To the extent that it is reasonably possible, punishment might well be the natural consequence of the act. It is important that the student sense this cause and effect relationship. Growth in freedom cannot readily take place without opportunity for making decisions in situations wherein the consequences can be at least partially foreseen.

28. "Be sure that punishment makes children better, not bitter." (Gruenberg)

29. Avoid using school work as punishment because of the simultaneous learnings in the form of negative attitudes which interfere with further learning.

30. "Remember that the child is in trouble, not that he is a trouble to you." (Gruenberg)

31. The teacher's personality has a marked influence upon his effectiveness in directing students. You can improve your personality.

Nature of Standards   Closely related to the foregoing, and especially to Number 15 is the importance of recognizing the real nature of standards of achievement. Standards, worthy of the name, are not the arbitrary figmentation of a dictatorial teacher's whim or wishful thinking. They represent average accomplishments of large numbers of pupils of a given age or stage of development, to be exceeded by some pupils and not expected fully of some others. Individual adaptations of standards in the light of abilities and backgrounds need to be made intelligently by teachers and pupils. It, unfortunately, often happens that some bright children have lower achievement quotients (accomplishment in relation to ability to achieve) than do certain so-called slow children because of being content with only standard accomplishment while certain slow children are being frustrated and discouraged by being held to the same standard. Blanket, stereotyped, uniform assignments, under an antedated, artificial system of lesson assigning and lesson hearing, are responsible for creating and aggravating problems. Intelligently creative teachers recognize that standards really function as suggestive standards of expectancy to be applied with discretion to individual pupils so as to encourage greater and more lasting progress. Instructional standards are false unless they are arranged in accordance with the natures and maturation levels of those to be served.

Understanding the Individual Child.   A serious lack of understanding of certain pupils by teachers in years past and gross misapplication of the above, along with other factors, including the rigidity of many uninteresting and unsympathetic schools, resulted in the following being expelled from school for supposed "inability to learn."[2] The reader will recognize many of them:

Table VI
Expelled from School for Inability to Learn

Linneaus	Charles Darwin
Napoleon	Oliver Goldsmith
William H. Seward	Priestley
Patrick Henry	Richard Wagner
Sir Isaac Newton	Goethe
Samual Johnson	Henry Ward Beecher
Dean Swift	Pasteur
Wordsworth	William Cullen Bryan
Robert Fulton	Thackeray
Alexander von Humbolt	Daniel Webster
George Eliot (Mary Ann Evans)	Gladstone
Sir Walter Scott	Madam Curie
Lord Byron	Von Liebig
Huxley	Baron Robert Clive
Herbert Spencer	James Russell Lowell

It is reported that James Russell Lowell was at one time expelled from Harvard College for "inability to write English themes." The list could be considerably expanded if one were to accept mere rumors, but a written record has been available clearly recording the supposed reason in the case of each of the above. Most of them, of course, did not stay expelled.

The reader must not jump to the conclusion that all the great people of the earth have been expelled from school for inability to learn. The list not so expelled would be many times longer, but the tragedy is that people like the above could ever have been so badly misunderstood as to be thought dull in school when their potential creativity

2. The writer is indebted for this list to Dr. J. R. Jewell, formerly Dean of the Schools of Education of the State of Oregon.

was not being touched by the school. We should be at a much better advantage in our modern schools of today, but we should searchingly ask ourselves if we are letting potential genius or near genius slip by unawakened while we are literally making life miserable for certain others for whom uniform standards are not fitted.

In interpreting Pestalozzi, Messenger[3] makes the following interesting statement:

"When food does not agree with the baby, we change the food, we do not throw away the baby. When a doctor finds that his medicine does not help his patient he tries changing medicine rather than changing patients. If the instruction we give does not improve Johnny what should we do? Try to find something which will help Johnny or send him home and look for another pupil who will be helped by our instruction? Pestalozzi took the former course. . . . It is our job to find out what will benefit the pupils most, not to find out which pupils can swallow greatest amount of our curriculum."

Secondary Schools   The secondary school developed typically as a departmentalized school offering required courses and elective courses by teachers who had specialized in certain subjects. In addition there developed on a sort of "extra" basis what came to be called extra-curricular activities. An interesting part of the history of education has been the transition of certain so-called extra-curricular areas into curricular offerings. Extra curricular activities ought actually to be designated by the name, extra instructional or some similar term, inasmuch as the school curriculum is really composed of all the experiences of pupils in relation to their school life, and the school cannot safely ignore its responsibilities in relation to any of these experiences and special services in

---

3. Messenger: An Interpretative History of Education, p. 184.

the fields of counseling, health, recreation, etc.

In recent years there has been a tendency in the secondary schools to partially modify the more extreme departmentalization so as to make it possible for each pupil to remain with some one teacher for a longer period and to provide for an interrelated area of work, cutting across more than one subject, which some have designated as a core area.

In many of our better modern junior high schools the pupils engage in interrelated, coordinated school work under one versatile teacher for approximately a half-day, with the program departmentalized under various teachers for the remaining half-day. In large schools under highly departmentalized programs for the full day there have been many pupils whom no one teacher has known well enough to know and understand their problems, idiosyncracies, strengths, special interests, or peculiar needs. The combination program referred to gives evidence of strength in relation to this problem and carries promise of helpful integration for the pupils.

Elementary Schools   The preferred form of organization for the elementary school is the self contained classroom unit in which the pupils of a given group remain for the full day under the direction of one capable, versatile teacher who comes to know each child very well and who is in a postion to coordinate the entire range of learning activities in relation to child life and needs so as to provide for an optimum of integration or balanced growing. This type of organization recognizes no distinction between regular and so-called special subjects or areas. They are all regular including the music and art to which the regular room teacher gives attention with the guiding help of the supervisor. The modern program of teacher education provides the regular elementary teacher with preparation in public school art, public school music, physical education, etc., as well as in other phases of elementary teaching. The elementary teacher must be a specialist in child growth in relation to the entire program.

Extensive research highly favors this form of organization and strongly opposes the departmentalized, platoon type of organization which came in vogue a few decades ago for elementary schools and which has since been largely supplanted by the modern non-departmentalized school with self contained classroom units. [4] [5] [6] [7] Annual rather than semi-annual promotions or transfers from level to level are usually preferred. It is often found advisable for a teacher to continue to guide the development of the same group of boys and girls for more than one year.

One of the most significant advantages of the self contained classroom unit appears to be the greater freedom from emotional maladjustment on the part of the children in this form of organization as compared with those working under a plan in which the children change from teacher to teacher at designated intervals during the school day.

A study of promotions and retentions over a thirty year period reveals a tendency to retain an objectionably higher percentage of pupils in the platoon schools than in the nondepartmentalized elementary schools. [8]

Emphasis is placed on opportunities for all the children of all the people, and whenever programs are presented for the public all the children are featured rather than just a specially talented favored few. It is important for all children to receive development through well-rounded activities, including creative expression

4. Law, Reuben D., Content and Critera Relating to Professional Teacher Education, University of Southern California, 1941. Chapters 11 and 12.
5. Lee and Lee. The Child and his Curriculum. D. Appleton Century, 1940. Pages 176 ff. and 198. (Also 1950 edition)
6. Caswell, Hollis L., Education in the Elementary School. American Book Company, 1942. Chapter X (Especially pages 228-229) (Also recent edition by Caswell and Foshay)
7. Saucier, W. A. Theory and Practice in the Elementary School. Macmillan, 1941, pp. 155-156; 448-450.
8. Olsen, Marion J. A Study of the Promotion and Retention Practices of the Elementary Schools of Utah. Master's Thesis, Brigham Young University, 1948.

Grouping   In the grouping of children it must always be recognized that the school exists for the child, not the child for the school. Generally speaking, each child should be placed in the group in which he will make the optimum of desirable, balanced growing for his stage of development. As among the teachers of a given school (either elementary or secondary), age-grade groupings are most commonly preferred, with special individual adjustments when advisable in relation to the principle expressed in the first two sentences of this paragraph.

Although still practiced to an extent in certain areas, so-called homogeneous, ability grouping did not bring the results which its instigators had hoped,[9] and it has been vigorously opposed by some educational philosophers as undemocratic. So far as scientific research on ability grouping is concerned, the results are at best inconclusive.

Within many individual classrooms there are temporary groupings for certain specific purposes. These groupings within a teacher's room possess the advantage of flexibility, are different for various types of activities, and may very informally and very easily be changed from time to time or be completely disregarded when occasion demands.

The teacher's obligation should be to the child at hand rather than to the teacher at the next succeeding grade level. Likewise, the school's obligation should be to the child at hand in relation to his needs and the needs of society without being stymied by controls from the next succeeding institution.

Secret Societies   In the operation of a few large high schools, secret societies have sometimes become a problem, and have usually been ruled against by boards of education as having no legitimate place in the free, public secondary schools of a democracy.

---

9. Refer Monroe, W. S. (Editor): Encyclopedia of Educational Research. Revised Edition. New York, Macmillan, 1950.

Reporting to Parents   During the past few decades there have been some very significant trends in the procedures and methods of reporting to parents involving a recognition of the principle that reports to parents should be regarded as neither rewards nor punishments, but as helpful guides to further progress.

These reports have come to be quite informal, couched in the form of helpful explanations, and usually accompanied by parent-teacher conferences. In many school systems the planned parent-teacher conference completely supplants the written report to parents.

It is recommended that the student of education become acquainted with some of the research in this field [10], [11], [12], [13], [14], [15], [16], [17] and examine some of the better modern systems of reporting to parents used by elementary schools and by secondary schools. In the light of considerations pertaining to the child's all-round development, many have contended that there is excellent reason for parents to report to teachers as well as teachers to parents.

Records and Reports   The management of efficient school systems and the possibility of making continuous evaluations and re-evaluations require that teachers and administrators periodically make various types of records and reports with accuracy and complete-

10. Clark, Ervin: A Study of Reports to Parents at the Brigham Young University Elementary Laboratory School. Master's Thesis, Brigham Young University, Provo, Utah, 1950.
11. Sims, Arch: A Study to Discover Parent-Teacher Attitude Toward the Parent-Teacher Conference Method of Reporting Student Progress in the Corrinne Elementary School of Box Elder County, Utah. Master's Thesis, Brigham Young University, Provo, Utah, 1949.
12. Hancey, J. Everett: An Evaluation of the Pupil Reporting System in the Elementary Schools of Ogden, Utah. Master's Thesis. University of Utah, Salt Lake City. 1946.
13. Strang, Ruth: "The Truth About Report Cards," **National Parent-Teacher**, Vol. 43, January, 1949, pp. 4-7.
14. Coulter, Kenneth C.: "Parent Teacher Conferences," **Elementary School Journal**, Vol. 47, March, 1947, pp. 385-390.
15. Ginsberg, Sadie D.: "Elementary Report Card Misfits," Records and Reports, Bulletin of the Association for Childhood Education International, 1200 Fifteenth Street, Northwest, Washington 5, D.C., 1942, p. 4.
16. Hood, Charles E.: "Reporting on the Whole Child," **The Nation's Schools** Vol. 39, No. 1, January, 1947, pp. 23-25.
17. Naegele, Raymond J.: "Achieving a Pupil Progress Report," The Phi Delta Kappan, Vol. 30, No. 8, April, 1949.

ness. Students of education will find it helpful in their preparation to become familiar with these records and reports, a number of which are listed below as follows:

Book inventories
Inventories of supplies
Equipment inventories
Records of supplies received and supplies used
Cash accounts, if any
Record of pupil enrollment and attendance
Monthly report of enrollment and attendance
Annual statistical reports
Anecdotal record
Permanent, cumulative record
Class log
School and pre-school census
Pupil transfer forms
Payroll report
Record of certification and professional advancement

It is recommended that students cooperate in obtaining access to forms available for most of the above so as to obtain a first hand acquaintance with them in group discussions and an understanding of their use in anticipation of actual service in the schools.[18]

BIBLIOGRAPHY

Caswell, Hollis L.: Education in the Elementary School. American Book Company. 1942.

Caswell and Foshay: Education in the Elementary School. American Book Company. 1950.

Clark, Ervin: A Study of Reports to Parents at the Brigham Young University Elementary Laboratory School. Master's Thesis, Brigham Young University, Provo, Utah, 1950.

---

18. A nearby school district and the State School Office are sources from which such forms might be obtained.

Cooperative Study of Secondary School Standards, Evaluative Criteria. 744 Jackson Place, Washington 6, D. C. 1950 ed.

Coulter, Kenneth C.: "Parent Teacher Conferences," *Elementary School Journal*, Vol. 47, March, 1947. pp. 385-390.

Douglas, H. R.: Education for Life Adjustment. New York. Ronald Press. 1950.

Ginsberg, Sadie D.: "Eliminating Report Card Misfits," Records and Reports, Bulletin of the Association for Childhood Education International, 1200 Fifteenth Street, Northwest, Washington 5, D. C. 1942. p. 4.

Hancey, J. Everett: An Evaluation of the Pupil Reporting System in the Elementary Schools of Ogden, Utah. Master's Thesis. University of Utah, Salt Lake City. 1946.

Hood, Charles E.: "Reporting on the Whole Child,"*The Nation's Schools* Vol. 39, No. 1, January, 1947. pp. 23-25.

Kelley, Faunce, and Welling: Your School and Its Government. National Self-Government Committee, Inc. 80 Broadway, New York 5, N. Y. 1945.

Journal of Education, A Test for the Teacher, February, 1947.

Law, Reuben D.: Content and Criteria Relating to Professional Teacher Education. University of Southern California, 1941. Chapters 11 and 12.

Lee and Lee: The Child and His Curriculum. D. Appleton Century. 1940 and 1950.

Messenger: An Interpretative History of Education. p. 184.

Monroe, W. S. (Editor): Encyclopedia of Educational Research. Revised Edition. New York, MacMillan. 1950.

Naegele, Raymond J.: "Achieving a Pupil Progress Report," The Phi Delta Kappan, Vol. 30, No. 8, April, 1949.

Olsen, Marion J.: A Study of the Promotion and Retention Practices of the Elementary Schools of Utah. Master's Thesis, Brigham Young University, 1948.

Saucier, W. A.: Theory and Practice in the Elementary School. MacMillan. 1941.

Sims, Arch: A Study to Discover Parent-Teacher Attitude Toward the Parent-Teacher Conference Method of Reporting Student Progress in the Corrine Elementary School of Box Elder County, Utah. Master's Thesis, Brigham Young University, Provo, Utah. 1949.

Spears, Harold: The High School for Today. American Book Company. 1950.

Strang, Ruth: "The Truth About Report Cards," *National Parent-Teacher*, Vol. 43, January, 1949. pp. 4-7.

U. S. Office of Education: Core Curriculum in Public High Schools. Bulletin 1950, No. 5. U. S. Government Printing Office, Washington, D. C.

Spears, Harold: Some Principles of Teaching. Prentice-Hall, 1951.

Spears, Harold: The Teacher and Curriculum Planning. Prentice-Hall, 1952.

CHAPTER VII

FINANCING ELEMENTARY AND
SECONDARY EDUCATION IN UTAH

Background
Principles
As a preliminary to studying this section on school finance, the student is encouraged to again read Chapter I noting especially those principles and items pertaining directly and indirectly to the financing of education.

"A comprehensive program of education can be offered at reasonable cost only where local administrative units are large enough to bring together in convenient centers sufficient numbers of children in each age group to justify employment of well-balanced staffs of teachers for both elmentary and secondary schools."[1]

The educational system, in order to render the kind of service (quantity and quality) for which it is intended in a democratic society, must be properly financed. Schools can neither become nor long remain good schools without adequate financing along with an attitude of support and active cooperation on the part of the public. The importance of efficiency and wisdom in the expenditure of funds in relation to educational needs is of course recognized along with the importance of wisdom and adequacy in the raising of school revenues.

A Service
of
Administration
One of the services of organization and administration to the educative process lies in the providing and administering of necessary funds and in the operation of appropriate budgets as an effective means of carrying on this service

---

1. Council of State Governments: The Forty-eight State School Systems, 1949, p. 52.

*High
Efficiency
with Moderate
Expenditures
Per Pupil*
Utah's schools are known for their favorable organization and for their efficiency in the careful expenditure of school revenues. They have achieved a very high comparative rating in educational accomplishment with only a moderate expenditure per pupil in average daily attendance. According to data available through the U. S. Office of Education, Utah's per pupil expenditure for current operation of elementary and secondary schools in 1947-48 was $179.40, within three cents of the national average of 179.43 for the same year. A year later 1948-49 (the last year for which official comparative figures are available as this is being written) the national average moved up to $197.65 while the Utah figure dropped slightly to $178.02 which is $19.63 or ten per cent below the national average expenditure per pupil in average daily attendance, and $47.98 below the average expenditure of the eleven western states. These figures include both local and state revenues for elementary and secondary education.

*Greater
Effort*
Because Utah has larger families and more children per thousand population than most states, with the children of the state attending school more rugularly and completing more years of schooling than do the children of most other states, Utahns must make a greater than average financial effort. According to research studies reported a few years ago with the use of 1940 expenditure data, Hughes and Lancelot[2] rated this state fourth from the highest in effort to support education, public and private. These authors reported that 5.53 per cent of Utah's total net income was spent for education in 1940.[3]

---

2. Hughes and Lancelot: Education, America's Magic. State College of Iowa Press, Ames, Iowa, 1946, pp. 66-70.
3. **Ibid.,** p. 70. See also U.S. Office of Education Bulletin 1940, No. 2, Chapter II, pp. 124 and 125 and Chapter IV, pp. 238-279.

Per Cent of
Income Spent
for
Education

Chase and Morphet also place Utah fourth from the top in effort as measured by ratio of public school revenue to total personal income, but their tables comparing the per cent of total income of the people spent for education in 1937-38 with that in 1947-48 are somewhat disturbing.[4] In 1937-38 Utah spent 4.4 per cent of the income of the people for public elementary and secondary schools, and by 1947-48 the expenditures for the same purpose had dropped to 3.1 per cent.[5] This means that, although school budgets are considerably larger in recent years than they were a decade ago, increases in school revenues have not kept pace, relatively speaking, with the increases in total income of the people. In other words, in their relative share of the total income, the school districts of the state have lost ground financially.

This is also true of the nation generally with the percentage of national income spent for public elementary and secondary education having dropped from 3.1 per cent in 1937-38 to 2.3 per cent in 1947-48. Mathematically speaking, this drop in ratio from 3.1 to 2.3 is approximately a twenty-six per cent drop in relative financial status, or income status, while Utah's drop in ratio from 4.4 to 3.1 amounts to a still more serious twenty-nine and one-half per cent drop in percentage of the total income of the state spent for elementary and secondary education. It is not expected that the expenditures for education will rise and fall in exactly the same ratio as the fluxuations in national or state income, but when there is a persistent lag over a period of years in the percentage of income spent for education such as the above figures seem to indi-

4. Council of State Governments. The Forty-eight State School Systems. Chicago, Illinois, 1949. Chart 5, p. 19 and Table 3, p. 177.
5. With the college and university included the two percentage figures become 5.0 and 3.8 respectively.

cate there appears to be real cause for concern on the part of all who sense the importance of eduction.[6]

The reader should perhaps again be reminded that. with a per capita income near the national average and with a ratio of children per unit of population exceeded by only one other state,[7] the people of Utah must expect to put forth a relatively high degree of financial effort in order to maintain good schools, and they evidently desire to do so if one can judge by past records.

Biased Propaganda — Certain selfish interest groups as opponents of school revenue measures have repeatedly publicized direct comparisons between school expenditures today and expenditures during earlier years without at the same time showing the ratios between these expenditures and the total income of the people, and without showing differences in the size of the school population being educated as well as differences in price structures with accompanying devaluation in the purchasing power of the dollar, etc.

Constitutional Amendments — As foregoing parts of this volume have indicated, school revenues in Utah have been expended with great care and with exceptionally high effectiveness, and the people have, in the main, shown commendable interest in their schools. On five occasions between 1910 and 1946 inclusive the people of the state of Utah went to the polls and voted very substantial majorities in favor of amendments to the constitution designed to bring about greater equalization of educational opportunity throughout the state and better financing of schools. The dates of adopting these constitutional amendments and the funds established are as follows:

---

6. As an indication of society's ability to afford good education the reader may be interested in looking up the per cent of the national income which goes for luxuries of various kinds.
7. New Mexico.

1910   State High School Fund (Began at .5 mill and
        was changed in 1915 to .2 mill on the
        assessed valuation of the state).

1920   State District School Fund ($25.00 per census
        child).

1930   State Equalization Fund ($5.00 per census
        child raised and distributed according to
        an equalization formula).

1938   Uniform School Fund (No fixed amount speci-
        fied. Funds from miscellaneous sources,
        including escheats and forfeitures. Pro-
        vided needed flexibility in the law) (Dis-
        tributed according to an equalization
        formula).

1946   State Minimum School Program (Merged into
        one fund all the foregoing, preserving the
        Uniform School Fund; made it legally
        possible for the state to furnish up to
        seventy-five per cent of the cost of operat-
        ing elementary and secondary schools in
        the state on an equalization basis as de-
        termined by the legislature; dedicated all
        of the revenues from the state income tax
        and franchise taxes to the state school
        fund.)

The two amendments adopted in 1946 to provide the
constitutional basis for the minimum school program were
voted by the people by an almost four to one majority, a
remarkable indication of a desire among the people to improve and maintain good schools.

In connection with each of the above five occasions,
the preceding legislature set up the proposed amendments
in the form of joint resolutions (H.J.R. or S.J.R.) and provided for their submission to the people at the next general election. Following the adoption of the amendments by
the people, the legislature passed the necessary implement-
ing legislation in line with the mandate of the people.

Early
Territorial
and State Aid

Mention should also be made of earlier attempts to assist school districts through territorial and state aid beginning with an annual appropriation of $15,000 by the Territorial Legislative Assembly in 1874. The 1876 assembly enlarged the annual appropriation to $25,000 for public education, at least $20,000 of which was to be used in paying teachers, and the other $5,000 was to go to the normal department of the university for the preparation of teachers. The 1878 assembly changed the revenue law for territorial aid to schools and made provision for an annual three mill tax on the property of the territory, the funds from which were distributed to the school districts until statehood in 1896. It is interesting to note that a clarification of the law as early as 1880 clearly specified that the funds were to be distributed on the basis of the number of children in the districts between the ages of six and eighteen years.

In 1896 the chief features of the territorial school law were adopted by the state and a three mill tax for schools was perpetuated until 1915. The tax was then reduced to 2.2 mills and in 1919 it was raised to 2.4 mills, the proceeds from which went to the districts until, through the constitutional amendment of 1920, the State District School Fund, previously mentioned, was put into operation in 1921, providing $25.00 per census child between the ages of six and eighteen years as of October 31st, the official date of the annual school census.

Beginning in 1905 as additional help, small amounts of state funds were provided for the poorer districts which had great difficulty in paying their teachers salaries equal to specified state minimums.[8] The state appropriation in 1909 for this purpose was $8,000 for the biennium ($4,000 per year). In 1911 it was $10,000 for the biennium. It was raised to $15,000 in 1913 and to $20,000 in 1917.

---

8. See Moffitt: The History of Public Education in Utah, 1946, pp. 139 and 140.

Such aid was extended to poor districts until 1921 when the State District School Fund began operating as indicated above.

For a fuller and more detailed account of the development of state and district school finance in Utah the reader is referred to Moffitt's treatment of this subject.[9]

Minimum School Program   The student of education will be interested in the present method of financing elementary and secondary schools on an equalization basis under the state minimum school program made possible by the previously mentioned constitutional amendments of 1946 and subsequent legislation. The program of financing is worked out on the basis of classroom units with a specified amount of classroom unit support through the combined efforts of local districts and the state. The specified guaranteed minimum amount per classroom unit for operation of schools was set at $3300 by the 1947 legislature and the figure remains the same until changed by legislative enactment. The 1951 legislature passed legislation to raise the amount per classroom unit to $3600 but the measure was vetoed by the governor. Some supplemental aid was provided by special session legislation in the summer of 1951 for the poorer districts who levy a local tax of more than eight mills beyond the taxation required for the minimum program.

The classroom unit is defined in the law as 30 weighted pupils, and school districts are credited with classroom units under the plan in the following ways: (1) one classroom unit for each 30 elementary pupils in average daily attendance, (2) one unit for each 50 kindergarten pupils in average daily attendance (for example, 25 in the morning and 25 in the afternoon), (3) one classroom unit for each 20 pupils in average daily attendance

---

9. *Ibid.*, Chapter IX, pp. 117-151.

in junior or senior high schools,[10] (4) one classroom unit for each one-room school approved by the State Board of Education, (5) two classroom units for each two-room school approved by the State Board of Education,[11] (6) up to one classroom unit per teacher in similarly approved special schools so situated as to make it unreasonable to maintain the specified ratios and still provide an acceptable school offering, (7) one classroom unit for one full-time certificated professional, non-teaching person (ordinarily the superintendent), (8) one-half unit for each such additional employee such as assistant superintendents, supervisors, supervising principals, counselors, coordinators, etc. with proportionate allowances provided for part-time equivalents, and (9) one-third classroom unit for each vocational agriculture or vocational home economics teacher for each fourteen weeks such teacher is employed in an approved program beyond the regular school year.

It is just a matter of proper interpretation of statistics and a little arithmetic to determine the number of classroom units with which each district should be credited. The cost of the minimum program for each district and for the state as a whole is then determined by multiplying the number of classroom units by the amount set for each classroom unit by the legislature. To this total is added the budget for the State Board of Education and the State School Office as approved by the legislature plus an amount for pupil transportation ($675,000 per year alloted for pupil transportation from 1947 to 1952). This amount for the minimum program certified to by the State Department of Public Instruction to the State Tax Commission is raised for the ensuing year by a combination of district and state taxation.

---

10. This does not imply that classes should be smaller in high school than in elementary school, but this type of weighting is used to recognize the extra costs involved in high school science laboratories, expensive equipment and housing for athletics, large auditoriums, etc.
11. There are very few one and two-room schools in the state.

A tax levy is determined which, when levied against the assessed valuation of the wealthiest district of the state, will raise the amount equal to the full cost of the minimum program in that district. This tax levy is then required as a local uniform minimum levy in all districts of the state, and in addition each district is entitled to receive from the state the difference between the cost of its minimum program as defined above and the amount such uniform levy will raise locally. For the state's part of the program, the State Tax Commission determines the state property tax needed for the funds necessary in addition to the state income tax, franchise tax and other miscellaneous sources of revenue listed in the law.[12, 13] The Uniform School Fund consists of monies received from (a) the interest on the Permanent State School Fund, (b) escheats and forfeitures and funds from the sale or other disposition of property accruing to the state by escheat or forfeiture, (c) unclaimed shares and dividends, (d) the sale or other disposition of timber, minerals or other property from school and state lands, (e) the United States under the Leasing Act of 1920, funds from which are allocated to this fund, (f) rentals derived from the leasing or renting of school lands and other state lands including forfeitures, penalties, grazing and other fees, etc. (g) state income tax and corporation franchise tax, (h) state property tax for school purposes, and (i) any other constitutional or legislative allocations to the fund which might be made.

The funds are distributed to the districts from time to time throughout the school year. As the money becomes available in the Uniform School Fund, the Superintendent of Public Instruction certifies to the State Auditor the apportionment to be received by each district.

---

12. School Laws of the State of Utah, 1949, 75-13 1, pp. 44 and 45 (also current edition).
13. The state property tax cannot amount to more than 75 per cent of the state's portion of the cost of the minimum program.

*Local
Leeway*
It would, of course, be a grave mistake if a minimum program were ever permitted to become the maximum program with no flexibility permitted on the part of individual school districts wishing to go beyond the minimum. The law, therefore, permits local leeway to finance beyond the minimum program to the extent of 7 mills or forty per cent, which ever is greater, plus an additional ten per cent "for purchase of school sites, the erection or remodeling of school buildings and for the equipment of the same."[14] To meet emergency conditions the law also provides that, with the approval of the voters at a special election called for the purpose, any district may increase its costs of operating schools in an amount not exceeding an additional ten per cent.

*Minimum
Educational
Requirements*
To be eligible to receive state funds a school district must meet the requirements of state law and the regulations of the State Board of Education which have the effect of law under authority granted by the legislature. Among these requirements are the following:[15]

1. A school term of not less than nine months.
2. The employment of legally certified teachers and administrators.
3. The transportation to and from school of all pupils living more than two and one-half miles from school, or reasonable provision toward such transportation.
4. General supervision to assist the superintendent and such supervising principles as the State Board of Education may approve.
5. The expenditure for educational supplies and equipment in such proportionate amounts as will provide for efficient instruction, the proportionate amount to be expended for such purposes to be determined by

---

14. School Laws of the State of Utah, 1951. 75-12-8, p. 52.
15. Ibid., 75-7-24 to 26, p. 15.

the State Board of Education from studies made annually under its direction.

6. Provisions for health inspection and instruction.

7. The providing of all required reports.

8. The filing of the district salary schedule annually with the State Board of Education on or before October 1st of each year.

9. Such other requirements as may be prescribed by law.

School Budgets   School revenues are raised and expended through the operation of school budgets which should be cooperatively built in relation to educational needs and the reasonable possibility of sources of revenue. A budget is more than a mere statement or account of how money has been raised and expended. Such a statement is, of course, helpful as a background, but a budget is a classified statement of planned revenues and expenditures for a given period. In a school district this is one fiscal year from July 1st to June 30th.

As indicated in Chapter V the superintendent of schools is the budget officer of the board.[16] He wisely seeks the cooperation of teachers, principals, supervisors, the clerk, and others in the making of the tentative budget which it is his responsibility to recommend to the board of education on or before June 1st of each year. The board of education on or before June 30th adopts the budget for the next fiscal year as recommended by the superintendent or as modified by the board, but before the budget can be officially adopted the law requires that the people be given opportunity to appear at a public hearing on the budget. Notice of time and place of said public hearing must be published in a newspaper of general circulation in the district at least one week in advance of the holding of such hearing. The law also requires that a copy of the

---

16. **Ibid.,** 75-21-1, p. 60.

proposed budget be placed on file with the clerk of the board and available for public inspection at least ten days prior to the holding of any such public hearing.

The purpose of the public hearing is to give interested citizens an opportunity to become informed on the proposed budget and to try to influence the board by registering either their support, opposition, or other suggestions if they care to do so. The board, however, is not bound by any vote which might be taken at the hearing which is not ordinarily a vote taking meeting. Sometimes the group appearing at the hearing is a fairly representative group, and at times the group is far from being representative of the people of the district, but they should certainly have opportunity to be heard. The holding of the hearing relieves the board of none of its responsibilities in the making of official decisions. It is still responsible to all the people of the district for the adoption of an adequate school budget to make possible a proper educational program for the district.

The above regulations regarding a public hearing also apply during the year whenever the board desires to increase the amount set up in any major division of the budget.[17]

School taxes are collected by the county treasurer and the State Tax Commission and turned over to the school district as provided by law.

All expenditures are to be approved by the board of education and are to be kept within the limits set by the budget. No member of a board of education may legally "take or be directly or indirectly interested in any contract for goods, work, transportation, insurance, services or in any other thing with the board of which he is a member" or with any school, part or division of the organization of the school district which he serves as a board member.[18]

---

17. **Ibid.**, 75-21-2, p. 60.
18. **Ibid.**, 75-11-9, p. 41.

Audit   At least once each biennium a complete audit of the books is required to be made by a licensed public accountant. The law requires that copies of the audit be filed with the school district, with the state auditor, and with the state superintendent of public instruction.

Funds for Sites, Buildings, and Equipment   The constructing and equipping of school buildings, along with the purchasing of sites, usually involves extensive financing beyond the scope of a single year's revenues included in the regular current budget. Such financing may be handled by the district in any of three ways: (1) through establishing and maintaining over a period of years a building reserve fund for capital outlay purposes, (2) through levying a special tax voted by the electors of the district for a period of one, two, or more years, and (3) by creating bonded indebtedness authorized by a majority vote of the tax paying electors of the district.

Building Reserve Fund   By passing House Bill 147 the 1951 legislature made it legally possible for any school district to create and operate a building reserve fund over a period of years. This has long been needed as a serviceable and convenient means of financing the erection of school buildings on a pay-as-you-go basis. Funds may be accumulated in advance and be deposited in a separate bank account to meet the capital outlay costs of the school district which may include the planning, construction, replacement, improvement, equipping and furnishing of school buildings and purchasing of school sites. Interest on the fund accrues to the benefit of the fund. Investment of the funds while being accumulated is limited to obligations of the United States Government or of the state of Utah or its political subdivisions which are redeemable within five years.

The board of education may allocate to this fund any revenues from the state which are made available for capital outlay purposes and such other revenues as the school district may raise locally for this purpose. Any surpluses in the district general fund may be placed in the building reserve fund. Whenever the board desires to expend part or all of this fund for the purposes mentioned above, a public hearing is required similar to the hearing mentioned in relation to adopting or increasing the budget and under similar regulations. Money from this fund cannot be used for purposes other than capital outlay as enumerated above.

Special Tax In addition to the authorization which was granted by the legislature to boards of education to raise funds beyond the minimum program to the extent of seven mills or forty per cent, whichever is greater, plus an extra ten per cent for building purposes, "any board of education may at a special election called for the purpose submit to the electors of the district the question of levying a special tax for one or more years to buy sites, build and furnish school houses, or improve the school property under its control; provided the amount of said tax shall not exceed one per cent of the assessed value of all taxable property in any one year in such district."[19]

Bonded Indebtedness To obtain needed extensive funds for immediate use for capital outlay without waiting for these funds to be accumulated over a period of time through regular or special taxation as indicated above, the law makes it possible for any school district within the state to go into debt by issuing bonds to the extent of not to exceed four per cent of the reasonable fair cash value of taxable property within the school district. Taxes are then levied over a period of time to redeem the bonds on an amortization basis. Such bonds cannot be issued, however, without a majority approval of the taxpaying qualified voters of the district at a special

---

19. Ibid., 75-12-12, p. 47.

election called for the purpose and conducted according to regulations specified by law.[20]

Approval of Plans and Specifications No school building or addition to a building can legally be erected in a county school district until the plans and specifications for such building or addition have been filed with and approved by the state superintendent of public instruction, except in the case of construction costing not to exceed $5,000.[21]

Need for Broadening Tax Base Criticisms have arisen in some circles because such a large proportion of the revenue to support education is derived from property taxes. According to a recent publication by the Council of State Governments,[22] the proportion of all school revenues derived from property taxes in Utah in 1947-48 was 74.9 per cent compared with a median for the nation of 60.5 per cent. Conversely, the proportion of school revenues from sources other than property taxes was 21.5 per cent for Utah compared with a median of 39.5 for the nation as a whole. As only one example of other possibilities there are those who point to the fact that Utah does not have a severance tax on vast extractions of minerals taken annually from the natural deposits of Utah, the greater part of which leaves the state. A 1947 publication of the State Department of Publicity and Industrial Development[23] reported that Utah is a leading state in mineral output, indicating that in 1945 Utah produced thirty per cent of all the copper produced in the United States, twenty-eight per cent of the gold, nineteen per cent of the silver, ten per cent of the lead, and five per cent of the zinc, and then added the comment that "No other area has a comparable record." There are also vast deposits of iron ore, coal, oil, salt, and

20. **Ibid.**, Chapter 13, 75-13-1 to 21, p. 48-51.
21. **Ibid.**, Chapter 14, 75-14-1 to 5, pp. 51 and 52.
22. Council of State Government: The Forty-eight State School Systems, Chicago, Illinois, 1949, pp. 117 and 225.
23. Utah Development News, Salt Lake City, Vol. 5, No. 8, September, 1947.

other minerals. Undoubtedly there are also a number of other types of possible sources for broadening the tax base. It is likely that future legislatures of this state will wish to increase the proportion of school revenues coming from sources other than property taxes as a means of balancing and broadening the base for adequate financial support of schools.

In 1947-48, $750,000 or 6.1 per cent of Utah school revenues came from permanent school funds and lands.[24] The permanent school fund was derived from land grants referred to elsewhere in this volume.

Conclusion As an appropriate conclusion to the foregoing material of this chapter the student will be interested in the following generalized statement of principles regarding state school finance:

Every state school finance program should:

(1) help to assure reasonably adequate and well-rounded educational opportunities for all children and youth throughout the state (equalization principal); and (2) be based on a system of taxation and administration which assures that the burden of support will be equitably distributed among all types and classes of citizens and taxing units. In addition to promoting these two major objectives, the best school finance practices encourage desirable local initiative and responsibility, promote bona fide economy and efficiency, and facilitate educational progress.[25]

BIBLIOGRAPHY

Council of State Governments: The Forty-eight State School Systems. Chicago, Illinois, 1949.

Mort, Paul R. and Reusser, Walter C.: Public School Fi-

---

24. Council of State Governments: The Forty-eight State School Systems. Chicago, Illinois, 1949. Table 50, p. 226.
25. **Ibid.,** p. 111.

nance. New York, McGraw-Hill. 1941.

National Education Association Committee on Tax Education and School Finance: Guides to the Development of State School Finance Programs. 1201 Sixteenth Street, N.W., Washington, D. C. 1949.

Phi Delta Kappa, National Commission on the Support of Public Education, Edgar L. Morphet, Chairman: Some Important Issues Relating to the Support of Public Education. 2034 Ridge Road, Homewood, Ill. 1949.

State Department of Public Instruction, E. Allen Bateman, Superintendent: School Laws of the State of Utah. 1951.

State Department of Publicity and Industrial Development: Utah Development News "Utah Leads Nation in Mineral Output," Salt Lake City, Utah, Volume 5, Number 8, September, 1947.

Utah Education Association: Dollars and Sense (Pamphlet) Salt Lake City, Utah. 1950.

U. S. Chamber of Commerce (Education Committee): Education, An Investment in People, Washington, D. C. 1944.

U. S. Chamber of Commerce (Education Committee): The Growing Challenge, Washington, D. C. 1950.

U. S. Office of Education (Morphet and Lindman): The Public School Finance Programs of the Forty-eight States. Circular No. 274. U. S. Govt. Printing Office, Washington, D. C. 1950.

U. S. Office of Education: Financing Public Education: General Features of a Satisfactory State Plan. Leaflet No. 78. U. S. Govt. Printing Office, Washington, D. C. 1947.

CHAPTER VIII

COLLEGES AND UNIVERSITIES

*Early
Attention
to Higher
Education*
Attention to higher education was given at a very early date in what is now the state of Utah. The pioneers arrived in the Salt Lake Valley in 1847 and began the colonization of this intermountain area. They applied for statehood in 1850 and one of the first acts passed by the Legislative Assembly of what they hoped would be the state of Deseret was an act passed February 28, 1850, providing for the incorporation of the University of Deseret from which beginning the University of Utah traces its origin (Congress in 1850 created the Utah Territory instead of the State of Deseret).[1]

*Ten
Colleges
and
Universities*
Today there are ten recognized, accredited colleges and universities in the state, seven of which are state institutions, one is a church university, and two are church colleges.[2]

*Financial
Support*
The state institutions are supported principally by legislative appropriations, several forms of federal aid, and student fees. The private institutions are supported principally by the churches that founded them, small endowments, and student fees.

*Governing
Bodies*
The governing bodies of the University of Utah and the Utah State Agricultural College with its B.A.C. and Snow College branches are the Board of Regents and the Board of

---

1. It is interesting to note that the orgainzation of the University of Deseret was patterned after the University of the City of Nauvoo established in Nauvoo, Illinois by Joseph Smith in 1841.
2. The 1951 Book of the States includes 1946 data regarding 1,768 colleges and universities in the U.S., 624 of which were public and 1144 private. (Council of State Governments: The Book of the States, Chicago, Illinois, 1951, p. 291.)

Trustees respectively. Each of these two separate boards consists of the secretary of state and the president of the respective alumni association as ex-officio members, and twelve resident citizens of the state appointed by the governor by and with the consent of the senate. Six of the twelve appointees are appointed each two years for terms of four years. No compensation is allowed to members of the board for their time or services, but they may be reimbursed for their actual and necessary expenses incurred in the performance of their official duties. The law also provides that the president of the university shall be ex officio a member of the board of regents.[3]

It appears to the writer, that, in terms of stability and continuity related to intellectual freedom so essential to educational institutions worthy of support by a democracy there is a serious weakness in the above arrangement which would permit a governor in the course of a single four-year term of office to name new members to all twelve appointive positions on the Board of Regents of the University of Utah and all twelve appointive positions of the Board of Trustees of the Utah State Agricultural College. Reforms should be instituted which would prevent such a possibility from ever occurring.

The governing body of the three state junior colleges is the State Board of Education. The governing boards of the private institutions are appointed by the respective churches that control and support the institutions. At each institution the governing board selects and appoints the president except that in the case of the state junior colleges the board appoints the president upon the recommendation of the state superintendent of public instruction. At each college and university the faculty members and other employees are selected by the president and appointed by the board upon his nomination and recommendation. Advancement in rank is also by approval of

---

3. School Laws of the State of Utah, 1949. 75-4-7 and 8; 75-5-9, pp. 21 and 26.

the board acting upon recommendations through the president. Under the president, the deans, department heads, and directors serve as heads of various divisions of the universities and colleges. Budgets must, of course, be approved in each case by the governing board.

Enrollment   For an indication of the budgets, fees, courses of study, enrollments, and administrative organizations of these institutions the reader should refer to the annual or biennial reports and annual catalogues of the institutions.[4]

According to a study reported by the U. S. Office of Education regarding the 1,859 institutions of higher education in the forty-eight states and the district of Columbia, 2,535,265 students were enrolled in the colleges and universities in 1949-50 including 28,662 from foreign countries, 7,058 from outlying areas, and 1,273 students whose states of residence were not specified. The 2,486,-396 students, not including the latter three groups, were classified according to the state of home residence and the state of attendance at school.[5] There were 24,390 of these attending higher institutions in Utah,[6] 78.6 per cent of whom were residents of Utah and 21.4 per cent residents of other states.

According to the report, 20,865 residents of Utah were attending higher institutions in the United States, of whom 91.9 per cent were attending institutions in their home state of Utah and 8.1 per cent were attending school in other states. The excess of student migration into the state of Utah over the migration of students out of the sate in 1949-50 was 3,525. These figures include all higher institutions both public and private.

---

4. Utah has a significantly greater per cent of its population attending colleges and universities than has any other state or nation.

5. "Geography of College Students," Higher Education, Vol. VII, No. 11, February 1, 1951, pp. 124 and 125.

6. The figure is somewhat higher when students from the territories and foreign countries are added.

*Instruction
in the U. S.
Constitution*
State law requires that there be given regular courses of instruction in the constitution of the United States in all public and private schools including colleges and universities, located within the state.[7]

*No Partisan
or
Denominational
Doctrine as
Qualification*
In the state supported institutions it is unlawful to teach "any partisan political, atheistic, infidel, sectarian-religious or denominational doctrine," and no political or religious test can be required or religious or political partiality or preference shown in the appointment of the faculty or other employees.[8]

*Out of
State
Fees*
In addition to the regular tuition and other fees chargeable against residents of the state, the state supported university and colleges are required by law to charge an out-of-state fee of not less than thirty-five dollars per quarter to those students whose domicile is not in the state of Utah, provided that such fee "may be remitted in whole or in part in the case of graduate students and in the case of students in attendance at a summer school."[9]

*Teacher
Education
and
Certification*
By legislative enactment, the College of Education of the University of Utah is the State School of Education, but all of the higher institutions of the state contribute in some measure to the education of teachers. University of Utah, Utah State Agricultural College, Brigham Young University, St. Mary of the Wasatch, and Westminster College are recognized as recommending institutions to the State Department of Public Instruction for the issuing of teacher's certificates. Each of the first three named institutions have a full-fledged school or college of education and a graduate program

---

7. School Laws of the State of Utah, 1949. 75-1-1 and 2, pp. 16 and 17.
8. Ibid., 75-1-4, p. 17.
9. Ibid., 75-2-1, p. 19.

through which administrators and supervisors as well as teachers may qualify for certificates upon the recommendation of the dean of the respective school or college of education.

Variety of Study Fields The higher institutions of the state provide extensive preparation in a wide variety of fields too numerous to be enumerated in detail here.

History and Present Status The reader is encouraged to become familiar with the history and present status of each of the higher institutions of the state by referring to the annual catalogue and other publications of each institution. These should be on file in the library. For the convenience of the reader in looking up these materials, the names and locations of the ten colleges and universities of the state are listed below, classified as to state and private institutions:

State Institutions

University of Utah, Salt Lake City
Utah State Agricultural College, Logan
Branch Agricultural College, Cedar City
Snow Branch of Utah State Agricultural College, Ephraim
Weber College, Ogden
Dixie College, St. George
Carbon College, Price

Private Institutions

Brigham Young University, Provo
St. Mary of the Wasatch, Salt Lake City
Westminster College, Salt Lake City

BIBLIOGRAPHY

Benjamin, Harold et.: Democracy in the Administration of Higher Education. Tenth Yearbook, John Dewey Society. Harper and Brothers. 1950

Council of State Governments: The Book of the States. p. 291. Chicago, Illinois. 1951.

Dixon, H. A.: "The Presidents' Commission on Higher Education," Junior College Journal, Vol. XVII, No. 9, May, 1947. pp. 372-375.

Bateman, E. Allen, State Superintendent of Public Instruction: School Laws of the State of Utah, Salt Lake City, Utah. 1951.

U. S. Office of Education: Higher Education Division: "Geography of College Students," "Higher Education, Vol. VII, No. 11, Washington, D. C., February 1, 1951.

U. S. Office of Education: Statistics of Land-Grant Colleges and Universities. Bulletin 1950, No. 11. U. S. Government Printing Office, Washington, D. C.

U. S. Office of Education: Toward Better College Teaching. Bulletin 1950, No. 13. U. S. Government Printing Office, Washington, D. C.

Utah Public School Directory, State Department of Public Instruction, 223 State Capitol, Salt Lake City, Utah. Latest edition.

CHAPTER IX

TEACHER RETIREMENT

*Founding
of
Retirement
System*
All of the forty-eight states have some form of state teachers' retirement system. The Utah State Teachers' Retirement System was established through legislative enactment in 1937 with certain subsequent amendments. The retirement system became effective July 1, 1937. All records and assets of the previously existing Utah Teachers' Retirement and Disability Benefits Association were transferred as of that date to the Utah State Teachers' Retirement System.

*Retirement
Board*
Provision was made for the retirement system to be managed exclusively by the retirement board, consisting of the superintendent of public instruction, the attorney general, two persons to be appointed by the governor, and three persons elected under the supervision of the retirement board from and by the active members of the system, not including retired persons.

The term of office of the five members other than the ex officio members is five years, one term expiring each year. The board chooses one of its own members as president, and employs a full time secretary, a consulting actuary, clerical assistants, and such other help as may be necessary. The members of this board serve without compensation, but are entitled to reimbursement for traveling expenses incurred in connection with membership on the retirement board.

The retirement board has the sole power and authority to hear and determine all facts pertaining to applications for benefits under the program and all matters pertaining to the administration of the retirement system. The board is required by law to meet at least once every three months, and may authorize its secretary to perform between meetings routine acts such as retirement of members and fixing retirement allowances necessary in the administration of the system in accordance with the provisions of the retirement law and the rules and regulations of the board, such acts of the secretary being subject to review and ratification, modification, or reversal by the board at its next meeting.

Retirement Fund   The retirement fund is made up of (a) the contributions of the members in the form of salary deducations, (b) appropriations from the general funds by the legislature, and (c) returns from investing the funds under regulations established by law. The retirement board has control of the administration of the fund except that the commissioner of finance with the approval of the governor makes all investments from the fund after the retirement board determines the amount or proportion of the fund to be invested, and the state treasurer is the custodian responsible for the safe keeping of the fund, including all monies, bonds, and securities.

Contributions by Members   The rates of contribution of the members adopted as a graduated scale by the retirement board from actuarial studies are based on sex and age at the time of entering the system. The younger members have on the average more years remaining in which to make contributions to build up the fund and hence the rates are lower for them than for those who begin at an older age. Conversely, the older the teacher at the time of entering the retirement system the higher the rate of salary deductions required. The rates are applied to each payroll on salary up to but not exceeding $2,500 per year. The rates in effect during recent years including the school year 1950-51 are given in Table VII.

Table VII
UTAH STATE TEACHERS RETIREMENT SYSTEM[1]

Members' Rates of Contributions in Percentage of Salary Effective 7-1-43

Exact Age	MALE Exact	¼	½	¾	FEMALE Exact	¼	½	¾	Exact Age
20	7.31	7.31	7.30	7.30	8.35	8.34	8.34	8.33	20
1	7.29	7.29	7.28	7.28	8.33	8.32	8.32	8.31	1
2	7.27	7.27	7.26	7.26	8.31	8.30	8.30	8.29	2
3	7.25	7.25	7.24	7.24	8.29	8.28	8.28	8.27	3
4	7.23	7.23	7.22	7.22	8.27	8.26	8.26	8.25	4
5	7.21	7.21	7.20	7.20	8.25	8.24	8.24	8.23	5
6	7.19	7.19	7.19	7.18	8.23	8.22	8.22	8.21	6
7	7.18	7.18	7.18	7.18	8.21	8.21	8.20	8.20	7
8	7.18	7.18	7.18	7.18	8.20	8.20	8.20	8.19	8
9	7.18	7.18	7.18	7.18	8.19	8.19	8.19	8.19	9
30	7.18	7.18	7.18	7.18	8.19	8.19	8.19	8.19	30
1	7.18	7.18	7.18	7.18	8.19	8.19	8.19	8.19	1
2	7.19	7.19	7.19	7.19	8.20	8.20	8.20	8.21	2
3	7.20	7.20	7.20	7.20	8.21	8.21	8.21	8.21	3
4	7.21	7.21	7.22	7.23	8.22	8.23	8.23	8.24	4
5	7.24	7.24	7.25	7.25	8.24	8.24	8.25	8.26	5
6	7.26	7.26	7.27	7.27	8.27	8.28	8.28	8.29	6
7	7.28	7.28	7.29	7.30	8.29	8.29	8.30	8.31	7
8	7.31	7.31	7.32	7.33	8.32	8.33	8.34	8.35	8
9	7.34	7.35	7.36	7.37	8.36	8.37	8.38	8.39	9
40	7.38	7.38	7.39	7.40	8.40	8.41	8.42	8.43	40
1	7.41	7.42	7.43	7.44	8.44	8.45	8.46	8.47	1
2	7.45	7.45	7.45	7.47	8.48	8.49	8.50	8.52	2
3	7.48	7.49	7.50	7.51	8.53	8.54	8.56	8.58	3
4	7.52	7.53	7.54	7.55	8.59	8.60	8.62	8.64	4
5	7.56	7.57	7.58	7.60	8.65	8.67	8.69	8.70	5
6	7.61	7.62	7.63	7.65	8.72	8.74	8.76	8.77	6
7	7.66	7.67	7.68	7.70	8.79	8.81	8.83	8.84	7
8	7.71	7.72	7.73	7.75	8.86	8.88	8.90	8.92	8
9	7.76	7.77	7.78	7.80	8.94	8.96	8.98	9.00	9
50	7.81	7.82	7.84	7.86	9.02	9.05	9.07	9.09	50
1	7.87	7.88	7.89	7.90	9.11	9.14	9.17	9.19	1
2	7.92	7.94	7.95	7.96	9.21	9.24	9.26	9.28	2
3	7.98	8.00	8.01	8.02	9.30	9.33	9.36	9.38	3
4	8.04	8.06	8.07	8.08	9.40	9.43	9.46	9.48	4
5	8.10	8.12	8.13	8.14	9.50	9.53	9.56	9.58	5
6	8.16	8.18	8.19	8.20	9.60	9.63	9.66	9.68	6
7	8.22	8.24	8.26	8.27	9.70	9.73	9.76	9.97	7
8	8.29	8.31	8.33	8.34	9.81	9.84	9.87	9.90	8
9	8.36	8.38	8.39	8.41	9.92	9.95	9.98	10.00	9

1. Information supplied May 24, 1951 by Ray L. Lillywhite, Secretary-Director, Utah State Teachers' Retirement Board, 203 State Capitol, Salt Lake City, Utah.

The retirement board is required under the law to have brought up to date at least each six years the actuarial investigations on which the rates are based.

Appropriations
by State
The state made legislative appropriations toward the coverage, for retirement purposes, of prior service rendered in the public schools of Utah by members of the system prior to the time the retirement system went into effect. This made it possible to get the system into operation under a plan which would not leave the older teachers of many years service without reasonable retirement allowances. The continuing obligation of the state to the state teacher retirement system is indicated by the following excerpts from state law:

From and after July 1, 1941, there shall be paid from the general fund in the state treasury, monthly, to the Utah state teachers' retirement fund a sum equal to 5 per cent of the total compensation paid to members of the retirement system for services rendered during the preceding month, and there is hereby appropriated from said general fund annually such amount as may be required by the provisions of this paragraph.

The retirement board shall certify to the state auditor at the end of each month the total amount of the compensation paid all members of the retirement system for services rendered to the employer since the last previous report and the state auditor shall thereupon transfer 5 per cent of the amount so reported from the general fund to the Utah state teachers' retirement fund.[2]

At the time of going to press with this account the state is seriously in arrears in meeting its obligations to the retirement fund because of inadequate legislative ap-

2. Utah State Department of Public Instruction: School Laws of the State of Utah, 1951, p. 86.

propriations to meet earlier commitments.[3]

Retirement of Non-Teacher Employees　　The legislature established in 1945 a retirement program for non-teaching employees of the public schools effective July 1, 1945, also administered under the retirement board mentioned above.

Membership Required　　All regular teaching and non-teaching employees of the public schools, including the state colleges and university, are required to become members of the retirement system except (a) teachers employed on a part-time or substitute basis, (b) teachers who are holders of retirement annuity contracts with the Teachers' Insurance and Annuity Association of America or other private organization in which the state of Utah contributes part of the premium, and (c) temporary exchange teachers from outside the state. Teachers classed in the above three exceptions are excluded from membership.

The employing school districts or institutions are required by law to withhold the salary of any employee who should be a member but who has failed to file information required by the retirement board under the provisions of the retirement law. School districts and institutions are required to cooperate with the retirement board in providing needed information and data and in remitting to the retirement board the required salary deductions of members of the retirement system.

Eligibility for Retirement　　Any member within two years after last rendering service may retire upon written application to the retirement board when he has at time of retirement been credited with fifteen or more years, or when he has been credited with fifteen or more years of service and has at-

---

3. "The State is in arrears to the Teachers' Retirement Fund by approximately $9,700,000 on the acturrial basis. It is approximately $2½ million in arrears according to the legal requirements which have remained in the Law." Quoted from letter received from Ray L. Lillywhite dated May 24, 1951 in response to an inquiry made by the writer.

tained the age of sixty of more years, or when he has been credited with thirty or more years of service and has attained the age of fifty-five years. Retirement is compulsory upon reaching the age of seventy regardless of service credited.

Retirement Allowance   The retirement allowance is made up of an annuity from the individual's contributions and a pension or pensions purchased by the contributions of the state, and is determined by a formula which is influenced by age, years of service, average salary for the last ten years, and a maximum placed on the state's contribution to the pension part of the allowance.[4]

The person being retired may, if he desires, elect at the time of retirement to receive a lesser monthly amount than he would otherwise get so as to have a beneficiary continue to receive benefits after his death.

Disability Retirement   After ten or more years of service, in case of physical or mental disability sufficient to incapacitate a member for continued service as evidenced from an examination by one or more physicians or surgeons selected by the board, a member may be retired on disability allowance in accordance with a formula provided in the law for this purpose.[5]

Withdrawal Before Retirement   When a person discontinues employment in a status requisite for membership in the retirement system and, therefore, withdraws from membership before retirement, he may draw out all that he has paid into the fund plus the accumulated interest on the part he has paid, but he may not draw on the part paid into the fund by the state. For the person who does not remain in the system until retirement the fund is really in the nature of a savings account with no loss to the individual.

4. For details see School Laws of the State of Utah, 1951, p. 88 or Teachers' Retirement Act (Bulletin), 1947, pp. 22 and 23.
5. **Ibid.**, p. 89 (Bulletin pp. 24 anr 25.)

Reentering After Withdrawal   If after presumably withdrawing permanently, circumstances change and a person reenters employment under the retirement system, he may redeposit in the retirement fund an amount equal to that which he withdrew. The redeposit may be in one sum or not to exceed six monthly or twelve semi-monthly payments. If a person upon reentering the retirement system does not make such redeposit he enters as a new member without credit for previous service as far as retirement is concerned.

Benefits to Beneficiary in case of Death   In case of the death of a member before retirement his beneficiary or beneficiaries, upon presentation of proper proof, receive (1) the accumulated contributions, including interest, of the deceased member and (2) an amount equal to one-half year's salary (the half year's salary is determined by the compensation earnable by him during the last six months under contract immediately preceding his death).

Local City Systems   Prior to the establishment of the state teachers' retirement system legal provision had been made for local teachers' retirement associations in cities of the first and second class.[6] With the establishing of the state system, provision was made in the law for coordinating and synchronizing these local retirement associations with the state system. At first members of these local retirement systems were permitted but not required to be members individually of the state system, but after some experience with this plan the law was changed to require that, "Every teacher who is employed in the public schools of this state on or after July 1, 1947, and who is a member of a local retirement association and is not already a member of the Utah State

---

6. **Ibid.**, Chapter 29, pp. 76-78.

Teachers' Retirement System, shall become a member of the system."[7]

In 1951 Salt Lake City, Ogden, and Provo teachers still had local retirement associations. Choosing to take advantage of the permissive legislation of 1949, an attempt was made to dissolve the Ogden system. The petition for dissolution voted by the membership was, at the time this volume went to press, awaiting further hearing by the State Supreme Court.[8]

Retirement Systems of Private Institutions The teachers of private institutions are, of course, not eligible for membership in the state teachers' retirement symtem but many of them are included in private retirement plans.[9] In the interest of time and space only one such plan is here mentioned. At Brigham Young University, for example, five per cent of the monthly salary is deducted from the pay check of each faculty member, and this is matched with another five per cent by the institution. Both amounts are deposited monthly to the individual credit of the faculty member with the Teachers' Insurance and Annuity Association of America where the fund accumulates and draws interest under a retirement contract with this company. Retirement is compulsory at age seventy and is optional at or after age sixty-five by request of the member or upon recommendation by the administration.

The size of the retirement allowance is dependent upon the amount of the individual's accumulated retirement fund, and the operation of a formula based on sex and on age at the time of retirement as well as on the type of option selected. The member may select to have payments continue during his life only or at a lesser

---

7. **Ibid.**, 75-29-29, p. 84.
8. The information regarding the present local systems was supplied by Ray L. Lillywhite on May 24, 1951.
9. Information regarding other plans may be obtained directly from the private institutions.

amount during the survival of himself and/or his beneficiary.

Members may at their option deposit extra amounts beyond the five per cent to their individual retirement funds, but these extra amounts are not matched by the university.

In case of death of a member before retirement his entire accumulated fund goes to his beneficiary.

In addition to the above mentioned benefits, the members of B.Y.U. faculty are also included in the program of Federal Social Security.

Retirement as Earned Income It should be recognized that in any equitable retirement system the retirement allowances should be regarded as earned income for service rendered during the active years of employment, and not in any sense a dole. Retirement provisions become part of the contract of employment (either stated or implied), and retirement benefits (although deferred) are part of the compensation for which employees are obligated to render service. These benefits are often a very important consideration in the decision to accept such employment rather than some other position.

Professionally and Sociologically Desirable It is also recognized as being professionally and sociologically desirable to have a means of honorably retiring members of the staff with an earned degree of security when they reach an age at which their effectiveness as teachers is normally decreased below that of earlier years.

BIBLIOGRAPHY

Laws of Utah, 1937. Chapter 85.

Remmlein, Madaline Kinter: School Law. 1950. Chapter Eleven.

Utah State Department of Public Instruction: School Laws of the State of Utah. 223 State Capitol, Salt Lake City, Utah. 1951.

Utah State Teachers Retirement Board: Teachers' Retirement Act. State Capitol, Salt Lake City, Utah, 1947.

CHAPTER X

THE FEDERAL GOVERNMENT AND EDUCATION

U. S.
Constitution
Although the Constitution of the United States does not deal specifically with education, thus leaving the control of education to the states, the federal government since the days of the Articles of Confederation has promoted the cause of education in various ways and in increasing amounts.

U. S. Office
of Education
The United States Office of Education was established by act of Congress in 1867 "for the purpose of collecting such statistics and facts as shall show the condition and progress of education in the several states and territories, and of diffusing such information respecting the organization and management of schools and school systems and methods of teaching as shall aid the people of the United States in the establishment and maintenance of efficient school systems, and otherwise promote the cause of education throughout the country."[1] The development of its organization and services from 1867 to the present time is an interesting chapter in the history of American education, but this material is too extensive to come within the purposes of the present publication. A recent reorganization was effected February 9, 1951 by Commissioner Earl J. McGrath in line with the form of organization shown in Chart II.[2]

The U. S. Office of Education is a division of the Federal Security Agency. The Commissioner of Education, as an appointee of the President of the United States, is responsible to the Federal Scurity Administrator for

---

1. Inside cover of School Life, Vol. 33, No. 5, February, 1951.
2. Letter of March 7, 1951, over the signature of Commissioner Earl J. McGrath and an accompanying Report on an Administrative Survey of the U.S. Office of Education of the Federal Security Agency by Public Administration Service, 1950.

Plan of Organization of the U. S. Office of Education
(Effective February 7, 1951)

the effective and successful management and promotion of the functions of the Office of Education.

The staff assistants indicated on the chart as directors are not intended to carry direct supervisory responsibilities, but their purpose is to provide information and assistance which will help the commissioner to discharge with effectiveness his responsibility for the administration of the office. The line of authority is from the commissioner to the assistant commissioners and their staffs. The three assistant commissioners are directly responsible to the commissioner of education for the successful and effective performance of Office of Education programs and services within theiir respective areas of responsibility. Whatever provisions are made for delegation of specific responsibilities, the final responsibility for the impact of Office of Education programs on the problems of American education rests with the commissioner of education.

Recommendation of A.A.S.A. The American Association of School Administrators of the National Education Association has recently recommended that the U. S. Office of Education be set up as a separate, independent agency governed by a national board of education instead of being subordinate to the Federal Security Administrator as at present. A recent resolution of the A.A.S.A. reads as follows:

"We reaffirm the position of the Association in urging Congress to establish the United States Office of Education as a nonpartisan, independent agency, governed by a national board of education. This board should be composed of representative laymen, appointed by the President with the consent of the Senate for long, overlapping terms. Such board should have authority to appoint the commissioner of education, who would serve as its executive officer.

"All activities affecting education at the national level now included within the jurisdiction of the Office of Education, or any which may hereafter be established or authorized by Congress, should be under the direction of the Office; and any attempt to weaken or lessen the effectiveness of the Office by the transfer of such activities to other departments, agencies, or bureaus shall be strongly opposed by this association.

"We pledge a continuation of our cooperation and support to the United States Commissioner of Education, Earl James McGrath, and the United States Office of Education."[3]

The writer heartily endorses the above recommendation. There is evidence that the Office of Education's efforts have in the past been unnecessarily and undesirably frustrated at times because of the position of the Office in the national set-up in Washington, a position not entirely commensurate with the dignity of its function in relation to American life. It is an oft repeated trueism that education is vital to a democracy. Nearly one-fifth of the American population attends school or college full time, and other millions attend part-time. Approximately one and one-half million persons were employed in the 1950-51 school year as teachers, supervisors, and administrators of education.

There has been too much of a tendency to administer many programs of great educational significance through specially created or already existing federal agencies other than the Office of Education. It is to be expected that in the nature of democratic government in a complex age many governmental agencies will become interested in promoting certain special projects of education related to their areas of principal concern, but in the opinion of the writer, all of these on the federal level, including the financial support for the same, should be coordinated through and directed by the Office of Education, sufficiently well equipped to perform this function with full and

---

3. Resolutions of the American Association of School Administrators, Atlantic City Convention, February 21, 1951. Also, resolutions at conventions during several previous years.

proper respect for state control of education within the states. This is far from the case at the present time as subsequent data in this chapter will indicate.

Appropriations for Education   According to the 1950 annual report of the Federal Security Agency, Office of Education,[4] Congress annually appropriates an estimated three and one-half billion dollars for purposes which are directly or indirectly educational. Thirty-four million of this amount, or less than one per cent, was appropriated to the Office of Education, thirty-two million of which was administered for two programs of grants-in-aid: (1) $26,977,882 in federal grants went to the states through the Office of Education in 1950 for vocational education of less than college grade; (2) $2,480,000 *Vocational Education* is appropriated annually through the Office of Education for federal support of colleges of agriculture and mechanic arts, and an additional $2,550,000 is supplied from the permanent Morrill-Nelson appropriation for instructional purposes in land-grant colleges.

Of the two million dollars for the operation of the Office of Education, approximately one-fourth was used in administering the programs of grants-in-aid, and the remaining three-fourths was devoted to services in the following major areas: educational organization and administration; methods of instruction; improvement of the teaching profession; international educational relations; collection, analysis, and publication of basic statistical information; and the over-all planning and administrative services essential to the work in all these areas. An extensive number of new bulletins, reports, and other publications containing useful information are available each year through the Office of Education.[5]

4. Annual Report of the Federal Security Agency, Office of Education, 1950. United States Government Printing Office, Washington 25, D.C., 1951, p. 32.
5. See "Publications of the Office of Education" obtainable at the U.S. Government Printing Office, Washington 25, D.C.

Research   In carrying on research the government has the choice of (1) establishing its own research institutions and processes and recruiting personnel for the same or (2) contracting with established research centers such as colleges and universities to do the work. In 1949 the total federal obligations for research development, including construction for research facilities, was approximately 1.2 billion dollars. Of this amount 96 million or about eight per cent was conducted by colleges and universities under alternative number two. Although the Federal Security Agency was one of seven departments and agencies contracting for research, no funds were appropriated to the Office of Education for use in contract research. Considerable research was, of course, carried on through its own facilities as part of its regular program.[6]

Veterans'   The Veterans Administration reports in-
Education   dicate that under Public Laws 16 and 346 an average of more than two and one-fourth billion dollars a year has been paid in educational benefits to veterans during recent years. The expenditure authorized for 1950 was $2,800,000,000 for an average of 2,158,-000 veterans who were using their educational benefits under the G. I. bill of rights. Of this number an average for the year of approximately 655,000 were enrolled in colleges and universities, 839,000 in schools of less than college grade, 644,000 in courses related to on-the-job and farm training. The Housing and Home Finance Agency, helping to house the veterans enrolled in higher education, has assisted in providing approximately 129,000 temporary housing units on or near the campuses. It is estimated that perhaps half of the veterans getting college training would not have been in college or university at all had it not been for the financial aid provided for the G.I.'s.[7]

---

6. Annual Report of the Office of Education, Federal Security Agency, Washington, D.C., 1950, p. 23.
7. Ibid., p. 24.

Military Education As a means of supplying junior officers for the armed services, the government helped to maintain training programs (ROTC - Army; AROTC - Air Force; or NROTC - Navy) in 231 of the 1,808 colleges and universities in 1950. The number was increased in 1951. The expenditure authorized for Officers' Reserve Corps programs for 1950 in both secondary schools and higher institutions was something over sixteen million dollars, not including the pay of from five thousand to six thousand military instructors assigned to the institutions.[8]

In the states of California, Maine, Massachusetts, and New York Maritime Academies are operated to train men for maritime service, and in 1950 these academies received a total of $1,053,492 through the Maritime Administration of the Department of Commerce. The federal government also provides for the operation of Federal Merchant Marine Academies, the Military Academy at West Point, the Naval Academy at Annapolis, and Coast Guard Academies. Approximately $15,836,573 was expended for these schools during 1950. Other schools operated by the federal government, and for which expenditure figures are not available as this material goes to press, include the National Police Academy, the Command and General Staff School, the National War College, the National Industrial War College, the Air War College, and the Air University. This latter group of schools is operated primarily for in-service training of the government's own personnel.

National Science Foundation On May 10, 1950, the President signed Public Law 507 establishing the National Science Foundation authorized to promote basic research and education in the sciences, particularly the physical, biological, and medical sciences, mathematics and engineering, both by initiating and sup-

---

8. Ibid., pp. 24, 25 and 27.

porting such research and by contracting to have such research done. Scholarships and fellowships may be granted in the fields mentioned. A special concern of the Foundation is research connected with national defense.

A National Science Board of twenty-four members is appointed by the President, by and with the advice and consent of the Senate. A director who is an ex-officio member of the board is appointed in a similar manner. Appropriations were authorized at not to exceed $500,000 for the fiscal year 1951, and not to exceed $15,000,000 for each fiscal year thereafter.

In his annual report of 1950, Commissioner Earl J. McGrath calls attention to the fact that "the Congress may well consider whether its necessary and desirable action in behalf of the natural sciences has not brought upon it the further obligation to act with similar effectiveness in the fields of the social studies and the humanities."[9]

Although recognizing the commendable purposes and great possibilities of the above program and organization, it occurs to the writer that it would be highly desirable, and in line with principles of good governmental administration, to have this entire program channeled for its support and administration through the U. S. Office of Education, but instead it was set up as a separate agency. This, of course, is true of many other programs as well.

Medical Education   The Public Health Service, a division of the Federal Security Agency, in addition to awarding research grants for the support of investigations of basic sciences important to health and the control of disease, provides fellowships and grants designed to encourage highly promising students to become more efficient in research in medical and related sciences. About $2,875,000 was appropriated for this program for the fiscal year 1950.[10]

---

9. Ibid., p. 26.
10. Ibid., p. 26.

The Veterans Administration has carried on a program of internships or medical residencies through which 2,456 men were acquiring experience and training to better fit them for the practice of medicine. For this program the authorized expenditure for the year 1950 was $8,247,-600.[11]

Extension Services   A number of departments and agencies have extension services each intended to serve a particular purpose. The Department of Agriculture, through the largest program of this type with a far reaching extension service organization, disseminates scientific and other information and provides demonstrations, etc., to keep farmers and their wives abreast of current developments in agriculture and home economics and to support 4-H clubs for young people. For this extension service $32,573,360 was available in 1950.[12] Mention has already been made of the $5,030,000 distributed each year to the land-grant colleges and universities through the U. S. Office of Education. Sizeable appropriations are also provided for agricultural experiment stations.

Aid to War Congested Communities   With the onset of defense preparations in connection with World War II with accompanying unusually rapid shifts and concentrations in population, the Lanham Act was passed to assist war-congested communities in providing needed facilities, including construction and operation of schools where such facilities were considered essential. After several earlier extensions of the program, the Eighty-first Congress in its first session continued the emergency program of aid to schools in areas disproportionately affected by federal establishments, and authorized an appropriation of $7,500,000 to be administered by the General Services Administrator.[13] In the second ses-

---

11. Ibid., p. 27.
12. Ibid., p. 27.
13. Ibid., p. 29.

sion of the Eighty-first Congress, legislation was formulated and recommended to put the program on a continuing basis in which the Commissioner of Education would be charged with the administration of the program.

Education for Children of U. S. Officials and Employees in Foreign Countries

In certain places where there are numbers of U. S. government officials and employees in foreign nations, the government assumes the obligation of helping to provide appropriate education for their children. In occupied countries especially this program has taken on considerable proportions.

Education in the Territories, Canal Zone, Occupied Islands and Isolated Projects

Various agencies, including the Navy, the Army, Department of the Interior, U.S. Office of Education, and other agencies, participate in the responsibility for education in the territories, Panama Canal Zone, occupied islands, and isolated federal projects. There appears to be need for better over-all coordination and centering of authority and responsibility in the administration of these programs.

International Educational Relations

Many departments and agencies of the federal government have some sort of international educational program . These programs are under the general supervision of the Department of State, but are administered in cooperation with other agencies and departments including the Federal Security Agency and the U. S. Office of Education. Under the Smith-Mundt Act and the Fulbright program there were in 1950 about 1,400 U. S. students, teachers, and professors going to other countries and about 1,600 students and teachers of foreign nations coming to this country for study.[14] Through the "Cooperation with American Republics Program" extensive educa-

---

14. Ibid., p. 30.

tional activities have been carried on in various parts of
South America by the United States. The Library of Con-
gress, with funds transferred from the Department of
State, has been especially active in this program.

Library of Congress   The great value of the very extensive Library of Congress as an important factor in
education and general enlightenment in this
country should not be overlooked. Especially
is this true in the case of the higher institutions which
have the benefits of inter-library loan service.

Education of American Indians   The education of the American Indians
is carried on through the Bureau of In-
dian Affairs of the Department of Interior
which for the year 1949 had available for
this purpose $12,054,000 for the operation of schools for
Indians, $1,664,000 for maintenance and construction of
schools for Indians, and $1,475,000 for operation of
schools for natives of Alaska. These funds have apparently increased in succeeding years. Nine thousand dollars
of the first figure was used to provide for tuition and other
assistance to American Indians in colleges and universities.[15]

A noteworthy development has been the increasing
utilization of the regular public schools for the education
of Indians in recent years. In 1947 the Bureau of Indian
Affairs had contracts with six states and more than 1100
school districts for the schooling of approximately 21,556
pupils.

Vocational Rehabilitation   Through the Office of Vocational Rehabilitation, Federal Security Agency,
with federal and state cooperation, there
is an extensive educational program provided to prepare
physically handicapped and partially handicapped persons to enter employment in the various vocations through
which they may become self-sustaining and render useful

---

15. Allen: The Federal Government and Education. McGraw-Hill Book Co.,
1950, pp. 36, 132 and 133.

service. In 1947 there were 21,941 persons who received training in educational institutions as part of this program for which the states paid $2,771,410 in tuition. The amount of federal money going to educational institutions for this program was $1,681,000 in 1947 and the amount available in 1949 was $2,207,000.[16] Readers who might know of disabled young people or adults who may be eligible for but not included in this program should send the information to the State Director of Vocational Rehabilitation, in care of the State Department of Public Instruction in the capitol of the state in which such persons are located.

Education of the Blind   For some time federal funds have been made available to promote education for the blind. According to the Council of State Governments $125,000 annually was made available for this purpose during each of the years 1948, 1949, and 1950.[17]

Loans for Housing of Faculty Members and Students   As a means of helping to meet the critical need for student and faculty housing on the nation's college and university campuses, Title IV of Public Law 475 which was approved April 20, 1950, made loans available on very favorable terms to the higher institutions. Up to $300,000,000 was made available for this purpose for administration by the Federal Housing Administrator under a plan carrying low interest rates and long term amortization which could, if desired and approved, be spread over as long a period as forty years.

War Surplus Commodities and Equipment   Over a number of years the government's program of disposing of surplus war-time equipment and commodities brought millions of dollars worth of

16. Ibid., pp. 34 and 82.
    1950-51, pp. 60 and 61.
17. Council of State Governments: The Book of the States, Chicago, Ill.,

such materials and equipment into the schools at a very nominal cost to the school districts and institutions.

School Federal funds, when matched by state *Lunch* funds, help to support a program of school lunches in public and nonprofit private schools under the National School Lunch Act of 1946 which was preceded by more than a century of sporadic and intermittent effort to provide satisfying and nourishing noontime lunches for children. This effort was greatly augmented during the depression years of the thirties. It also provided an outlet for dispensing many of the surplus commodities held by the government under its farm price stabilization program. The Secretary of Agriculture administers the school lunch program and apportions appropriated federal funds partly on the basis of population and partly in accordance with the relative financial abilities of the states. Up to 1951 matching by the states was on a dollar-for-dollar basis, but the law provided for gradual increases in ratio until 1955 after which the states pay three dollars for each federal dollar except that low income states are given special consideration by a formula which reduces their matching requirements by the percentage which the state per capita income is below the per capita income of the United States.

Federal expenditures of $83,500,000 were authorized for school lunch programs in 1950. Although not given administrative responsibility for the program, the U. S. Office of Education has been called upon frequently for advice to states and to schools in matters of nutrition education in relation to the school lunch program.

Land Grants and Very early in the history of our *Proceeds from* country, in fact, even before the *Lands for* adoption of the Constitution of the *Education* United States, the basis was established for federal land grants in support of education in the territories and in the states. It is very interesting and significant to note that while the country was operating under the Articles of Confederation, the Ordinance of 1785, in specifying the manner in which the western lands should be surveyed, specified that lot number 16 of every township should be reserved for the maintenance of public schools within said township. Soon thereafter the Ordinance of 1787 stated that "religion, morality, and knowledge, being necessary to good government and the happiness of mankind, schools and the means of education shall forever be encouraged."[18] The same year the Congress of the Confederation in selling lands in southeastern Ohio to the Ohio Company specified that section 16 of every township be reserved for schools and that two additional complete townships be reserved for the benefit of a college to be established at some later date.

With the admission of Ohio into the Union in 1802, the Enabling Act granted the sixteenth section of each township to the inhabitants for schools and a year later placed control of all school lands in the state legislature in trust for the purpose specified. Under the Ohio plan of 1802 and the Michigan plan of 1836 new states carved from the public domain until 1848 were granted one section in each township for the support of schools plus certain other specified amounts of land.

With the establishing of the Oregon Territory in 1848 Congress provided that the sixteenth and thirty-sixth sections of each township should be reserved for the benefit of schools in states to be created from the territory. By acts of Congress in 1850 and 1853 California was also granted two sections in each township. The Oregon plan of two sections prevailed until 1896 when Utah was admitted to the Union with a grant of four sections in each township as school sections for the support of education. In cases where any of the designated sections—2, 16, 32, and 36—had already been homesteaded or purchased by

---

18. Monroe (Editor): Encyclopedia of Educational Research. The Macmillan Company, 1941, "Federal Relations to Education," p. 495.

settlers, other sections as near by as possible were to be designated as school sections. The relatively long period of settlement under territorial status resulted in most of the choicest lands in the valleys already being taken up before statehood.

Arizona and New Mexico, admitted to the Union in 1912, received grants in accordance with the Utah plan.

The Oklahoma plan of 1907 provided for that state's public schools two sections in each township and a grant of $5,000,000 in gold in lieu of grants in the Indian Territory. An additional section in each township was granted with the proceeds to be divided equally among normal schools, agricultural colleges, and a university. Still a fourth section was granted for charitable and penal institutions and for public buildings from which aid has been extended to buildings in consolidated school districts.

The Morrill Act of 1862 provided for the grant of land to each state amounting to 30,000 acres multiplied by the number of senators and representatives in each given state, the proceeds to be used for the support of land-grant colleges of agriculture and mechanic arts.

It is estimated that approximately 145,000,000 acres of public land (222,562 square miles) have been received by the states from the federal government for educational purposes. These lands were to be used for the establishment of permanent school funds from which the proceeds only are to be used for current operation.

Beginning in 1802 the states have been given cash grants in the form of percentages of the net proceeds from the sale of public lands (recently five per cent) within the state. In 1836 the federal surplus was distributed to the states and a sizeable part of the $28,000,000 thus distributed was deposited in the permanent school funds of the states. Since 1908, by congressional authorization in that year, twenty-five per cent of the income from the National Forest Reserve has been paid to those states in which such income originated for the benefit of roads and public schools in the counties in which the reserves are located. Revenue from this source has gone to forty states and two territories. Similarly, since 1920 thirty-seven and one-half per cent of the income bonuses, royalties, and rentals received by the federal government from the extraction of non-metallic mineral deposits from public lands has been received by the states in which such public lands are located. A considerable portion of the amount has been devoted to education by the twenty-one participating states. A somewhat similar Grazing Act of 1934 provided for payments to seventeen participating states. In 1947 the sums of $4,546,723.96, $5,988,470.40, and $517,238.80 were received by the states from the last three mentioned sources respectively.[19]

The foregoing is not assumed to be a full coverage of federal participation in education. For a more complete listing the reader is encouraged to refer to the extensive and very inclusive table provided by Allen on federal education activities.[20]

The Issue of General Federal Aid to Education From all the foregoing material of this chapter it is very evident that federal aid to education is not a new venture. General federal aid to education is almost as old as the nation itself with land-grant specifications beginning in 1785. Beginning with the Morrill Act of 1862 appropriations for special types of education have flourished with increasing breadth and magnitude to the present time with accompanying specifications and regulations. With federal aid to education so entrenched in American life, with its related governmental organization and operation, one can hardly escape the conclusion that it is obviously a continuing, on going program.

The real issue seems to revolve around the principle

19. Allen, Hollis P.: The Federal Government and Education. McGraw-Hill Book Company, Inc., 1950, pp. 65 and 66.
20. Ibid., pp. 22-56.

of equalization of educational opportunity in a country of very uneven distribution of wealth in relation to school population, and around the related issue of whether further developments on the federal level should continue the expansion of ear marked funds for special purposes under federal regulation and supervision or whether the aid should turn in the direction of general appropriations for public education under the control of the states, with carefully worked out federal statutory provisions prohibiting the exercise of federal control and supervision. There is a real possibility that the longer the delay in reinaugurating general federal aid to education with prohibitions on federal control, the greater will be the tendency to move in the direction of expanding special areas of aid with federal supervision and visa versa.

BIBLIOGRAPHY

Allen, Hollis P.: The Federal Government and Education. New York, McGraw-Hill Book Company, Inc. 1950.

American Association of School Administrators, N.E.A.: Report of the Resolutions Committee, Atlantic City Convention, February 21, 1951. 1201 Sixteenth Street, N.W., Washington, D. C.

Council of State Governments: The Book of the States. 1313 East 60th Street, Chicago 37, Illinois. 1950-51.

Fuller, Edgar: "How to Avoid Federal Control of Education," N.E.A. Journal; 38: 362-63; May, 1949.

McGrath, Earl James: Annual Report of the Office of Education, Federal Security Agency, 1950, Washington, D. C., U. S. Government Printing Office. 1951.

Monroe (Editor): Encyclopedia of Educational Research, "Federal Relations to Education." The Macmillian Company, 1941.

Morphet, Edgar L.: "State and Federal Support of Schools," The School Executive, Vol. 5, No. 3, March, 1949.

National Education Association: The Facts on Federal Aid for Schools. 1201 Sixteenth Street, N.W., Washington, D. C., 1948.

Public Administration Service: A Report of An Administrative Survey of the U. S. Office of Education of the Federal Security Agency. 1313 East Sixteenth Street, Chicago 37, Ill. October, 1950.

U. S. Government Printing Office: (Bulletin) Publications of the U. S. Office of Education. Washington, D. C.

U. S. Office of Education: School Life (Magazine published regularly by the U. S. Office of Education).

CHAPTER XI

HOME—SCHOOL—COMMUNITY RELATIONS

*Reciprocal
Relationships*   A large part of what has been included
in other chapters has a bearing upon
public relations if one understands the
reciprocal relationship between the schools and the home
and community life. It has been said that life in the
schools should be an extension of the best kind of home
and community life. Conversely, the life of the home and
community is safeguarded, enriched, and improved by the
right kind of education.

*Community
School*   For some time the term, "community
school," has been in use as an indication
that the school should be a community center for adults as well as children, and that the school
reaches out into the environment and life of the community in its educational program.

*Importance of
Public
Relations*   The importance of the right kind of
public relations cannot be over empha-
sized. The schools belong to the people,
and a close, constructive relationship
with the people is highly desirable. Every school district
and every school as well as the profession as a whole
should have an intelligently planned, continuous program
of public relations with members of the community participating in the planning as well as in the program itself,
but this must be more than a mere veneer. It must have a
genuine foundation in good schools where there is effective
teaching which meets the needs of pupils and society and
in which there is open recognition of improvements made
and improvements needed.

However, doing good work in the schools is not
enough. There must also be an awareness of this good
work in the consciousness of the community and a determination to preserve and enhance it. There must be en-

lightenment through dissemination of pertinent facts, civic pride, and an attitude of support sufficient to withstand attacks made against the schools by selfish interest groups. People must understand that destructive attacks designed to undermine the schools are really attacks against themselves and the welfare of their children. The writer has great confidence in the good common sense and judgment of the people when they understand the issues involved and are possessed of the full facts in relation to those issues, but when their minds are clouded with propaganda in the form of cleverly selected partial information or even misinformation, there is real cause for alarm. The cure for misinformation is the effective dissemination of correct information in its full and proper setting by people in whom the public has confidence.

The Pupil and Public Relations   Our most effective and ever continuing public relations people are our students who are the direct beneficiaries or the victims of our good or poor teaching. A tremendously important and far-reaching means of insuring highly desirable home-school-community relations is to send every child home happy at the close of each school day with a feeling of satisfaction based on the fact that he is really being helped in making progress toward the achieving of his worthwhile purposes.

Professional Teachers   Capable teachers who render real service in a friendly and thoroughly professional manner, with great understanding, are, of course, indispensible. The writer once overheard his twelve year old son, who was confused with some sort of difficulty at school, say to one of his roommates who had come to our home, "Let's go talk with Mr. Hawkins; he'll understand." You may be very sure that the esteem with which Mr. Hawkins was held increased considerably in the mind and heart of the boy's father. A small incident you may think. No, a very significant incident in the life of a boy, which when multiplied many times becomes of great consequence in the lives of many students.

Well informed teachers as they personally participate wholesomely in the life of the community with their families, friends, and associates become an influence of no small importance in relation to the attitude of the public toward the schools.

Reports to Parents   Reporting to parents was mentioned in Chapter VI, but the significance of helpful reporting practices can hardly go unmentioned here. Such reports should be couched in the form of understandable, helpful guides to further progress, and not in the nature of rewards or punishments. Especially are the modern, planned teacher-parent conferences significant in home-school-community relations.

The P.T.A.   The National Congress of Parents and Teachers, with its regional, state, and local units, moves as a great constructive force in support of good public education. Its helpful influence has been widely felt, and only in very exceptional cases where its local offices have been misused have local meetings been turned into complaint societies in which individuals were invited to register public complaints against the teachers or the administration instead of constructively and cooperatively participating in planning for needed improvements as a group of parents and teachers in small group conferences as well as larger general meetings. Teachers should expect to participate in the work of this helpful organization as they move forward with their work for the benefit of children and youth.

The details of organization and operation are not reported here inasmuch as printed pamphlets containing such information are available for the asking.[1] These should be studied with care and may form the basis of a worthwhile report and interesting group discussion.

---

1. Communicate with your local, state, or national P.T.A. officers.

*National
Citizens
Commission
for the
Public Schools*
The National Citizens Commission for the Public Schools is a non-profit corporation for the improvement of the public schools. Its formation was announced May, 1949. Its members are U. S. citizens not professionally identified with education, religion, or politics. They reflect many different kinds of experience, serve as individuals and do not represent any organization or group. The Commission received initial financial support from the Carnegie Corporation and the General Education Board. It operates under the assumption that "the problems of public education concern all of us, and it is time for all of us to do something about them."[2] Two immediate goals are: (1) To help Americans realize how important our public schools are to our expanding democracy and (2) to arouse in each community the intelligence and will to improve our public schools.

A recent publication of this organization contains a tabulation of four hundred, forty-six questions about our schools which are very useful for study and conference purposes by local citizens committees and other groups.[2]

*The National
Commission
for the
Defense of
Democracy*
The National Commission for the Defense of Democracy through Education has a primary responsibility for investigating unjust attacks against the public schools. Their investigations have uncovered evidence of opposition organizations of national scope carrying the attack against the schools into every state in the nation, parading under deceiving titles and disarming claims, but with aims and objectives that work destructively against the American public school system. The names and identity of these

---

2. National Citizens Commission for the Public Schools: What Do We Know About Our Schools? 2 West 45th Street, New York 19, New York, 1950.

organizations can be had by writing to the commission office.[3]

N.E.A. Division of Press and Radio Relations   The Division of Press and Radio Relations of the National Education Association has been very active with considerable effectiveness. In addition to working directly through press and radio in reachin the American public, the division provides extensive help for state and local public relations committees in the form of bulletins and other materials and services.[4]

Avenues to the Public   The school paper, school district publications and reports, the daily press, magazines, periodicals, the radio and television, meetings and conferences, are all avenues which should not be neglected in meeting our obligation to keep the public informed as it has a right and need to be informed on matters of education.

Television and the F.C.C.   An event of great importance occurred when on, March 22, 1951, the Federal Communications Commission made the decision to set aside specified channels in the television area of the broadcasting spectrum for educational use. Eighty-two channel assignments in the very high frequency (VHF) area and 127 channel assignments in the ultra high frequency (UHF) area were reserved for noncommercial educational television stations.[5]

This did not just happen, but was the result of the cooperative effort of the Joint Committee on Educational Television, the members of which were National Education Association, American Council on Education, National Association of Educational Broadcasters, National Association of State Universities, Association of Landgrant Colleges and Universities, National Association of Chief

3. National Commission for the Defense of Democracy through Education, Richard Barnes Kennan, Executive Secretary. N.E.A. Headquarters, 1201 Sixteenth Street, N.W., Washington, D.C.
4. Division of Press and Radio Relations, N.E.A., 1201 Sixteenth Street, N.W., Washington, D.C. (See especially the PR Guide, 1951)
5. Farley, Belmont: Vision and Television, N.E.A. Journal, May, 1951, p. 357.

State School Officers, and Association for Education by Radio. The U. S. Office of Education also cooperated, but as a federal agency it was unable to have representation on the joint committee. The JCET employed legal council and presented seventy effective witnesses in nearly four weeks of hearing before the momentous decision was reached by the FCC. These television channels, although not the full number requested, provide a challenging opportunity for the forces of education. To assist educators in this important work the JCET was reconstituted on a permanent basis with the same organizations represented. It is financed by a large foundation and maintains a professional and clerical staff in Washington to promote the installation of noncommercial educational stations, give free legal and engineering advice to those interested in such installations, and to aid those who are producing and using television programs for educational purposes.[6]

Films   School officials and committees, P.T.A. and other groups will be interested in the following partial list of available public relations films:[7]

Education is Good Business—10 min. sound.
Presented by the Iowa State Education Association.

In one community business and industry proudly support their schools. In another community business and industry are less alert. The difference education makes shows up in better retail sales, larger magazine circulation, more telephones, more buying in general, and in a "more gracious, intelligent living."

Instructional Films—New Way to Greater Education— 25 min. sound. Produced by Coronet.

Demonstrates to the audience through many sequences from selected films how audio-visual teach-

---

6. Joint Committee on Educational Television (JCET), 1785 Massachusetts Avenue N.W., Washington 6, D.C.
7. Provided by Hartvigsen, Bureau of Audio-Visual Education, Brigham Young University, Provo, Utah.

ing saves time in presenting complex ideas, *saves money* by bringing costly equipment right into the classroom movie screen, and makes it possible for students to see familiar objects in a new light.

Who Will Teach Your Child?—24 min. sound.
Produced by McGraw Hill (National Film Board of Canada).

Film raises three important questions in the teaching profession; 1. How can we attract people of superior ability to teaching? 2. How should these people be trained? 3. Once trained, how can they be persuaded to stay in the profession and pass up more lucrative careers? Dramatic flash-back technique takes us into a series of classrooms where we see teachers in actual situations and watch them cope with the day-to-day problems of helping young minds in their development.

Pop Rings the Bell—23 min. sound.
NatSchServ.

"How technological developments resulting from the war, and the approach of the air-age is making, and will increasingly make new demands upon the schools of the nation, is the theme.

"Primarily directed to the American taxpayer whose dollars sustain our educational system. . .
Excellent for PTA groups.

Schoolhouse in the Red—42 min. sound. Color.
Sponsored by W. K. Kellogg Foundation. Encyclopedia Britannica Films, Inc. Witmette, Illinois.

Deals with the sociological and psychological factors involved when small communities face up to the problem of joining their school district onto a larger district.

Fight for Beter Schools—20 min. sound.
March of Time.

The story of how the aroused citizens of Arlington County, Virginia, raised their schools from the nation's poorest to a level that Dr. William A. Early, superintendent, calls "an educator's dream." The people of Arlington planned and worked to improve their schools. They voted money for more teachers. They erected new buildings. They expanded facilities by providing additional equipment. The film shows what every town can do when it becomes interested in its school problem.

Emphasizes the importance of an active and informed citizenry in getting better schools (Educational Screen).

Food For Thought—15 min. sound.
U. S. Dept. of Interior.

Illustrates effective planning, purchasing, preparing, displaying, and serving techniques utilized in the school lunch program.

Holtville, U.S.A.—16 min. sound. 20 min. showing time.

U. S. Information Service, U. S. Department of State. A description of a school and community working together.

New Schools for Old—10 min. sound.
Produced by March of Time.

Contrasts the little red schoolhouse, its methods and results, with the modern classroom and the effects of new teaching techniques.

Teaching: Mahnke—11 min. sound.
Produced by Vocational Guidance Films.

Briefly states the contributions of teachers to American democracy and presents the traits of a good teacher, the attractions in the teaching profession, the educational requirements, and the various types of teaching positions.

Collaborator says, "Takes a rosy view of things."

Teachers' Crisis—17 min. sound.

March of Time

The educational scene today is portrayed objectively for visits to America's classrooms and school board meetings reveal discontented and ill qualified teachers on the one hand and a disinterested community attitude on the other. Overwork and low pay are but two of the problems which have driven teachers to abandon the dignity of thier professions, to organize into unions and to go out on strike against conditions they consider no longer tolerable.

Kids Must Eat—17 min. sound.

Castle. U. S. Dept. of Agriculture.

Features the Quiz Kids. Their performance is worked into the film telling the story of the community school lunch program. Use of abundant foods in surplus and at the same time promote better nutrition to school children is the theme.

Community Coordinating Councils   The eight point program backed by the State Council on School-Community Relations in 1940, and referred to in Chapter III, contained the following as item no. 6:

"Effective coordination of the efforts of all community groups and organizations interested in and affecting the welfare of youth, such as the school, P.T.A., federated women's clubs, service clubs, civic organizations, etc. Organize and keep functioning community coordinating councils for the improvement of the local environment and most effective use of all educative resources and influences, all agencies including youth itself to be represented."[8]

Especially noteworthy examples of community coordinating Councils were found at an early date in Sandy and in Cedar City. Such councils have also functioned to advantage in quite a number of other communities. In some places they have been called youth councils. Is there a functioning community coordinating council in your community and what are some of the results? If not, why not, and what are some of the needed improvements that could be made by such a council or its member organizations?

Compulsory Attendance Laws   A most important way of contributing to a high educational morale in a school district is to properly account for every child of school age in the district with the right kind of educational program adjusted to meet individual needs. The great majority attend school voluntarily and we hope cheerfully, but unfortunately a few would drop out of school prematurely if there were not a program of follow up.

Compulsory school attendance laws were passed by the legislature as a safeguard to the individual pupil and to society. A wisecracker once said, "You can lead a horse to water, but you can't make him drink. You can force a boy to school, but you can't make him think." A very wise man replied, "You can lead a horse to water, but you can't make him drink unless you put salt in his oats."[9] Compulsory attendance enforcement protects the child against being exploited to his detriment, and gives the school its opportunity to work with the child who would otherwise be absent, but the real job comes in constructively helping him to meet his problems through wise guidance and in providing the right kind of educational program adjusted to his needs.

---

8. Law, Reuben D.: Community Councils in Action, 1941.
9. Dr. J. R. Jewill, Former Dean of the Schools of Education of Oregon.

The following excerpts are quoted from the statutes of the state of Utah:

Every parent, guardian or other person having control of any minor between eight and eighteen years of age shall be required to send such minor to a public or regularly established private school at least thirty weeks in each school year; provided that any minor under the age of sixteen years, who has completed the eighth grade or, being of the age of fourteen years and upward, whose services are required for the support of a mother or invalid father, or any minor over sixteen years of age, may be legally excused to enter employment, but if such minor is so excused, the parent, guardian or other person shall be required to send such minor to a part-time school or class at least one hundred forty-four hours per year; provided further that in each year the parent, guardian or other person having control of any such minor may be excused by the board of education of the district from sending such minor to a public, regularly established private or part-time school or class for any of the folloing reasons:

(1) That such minor has already completed the work of a senior high school.

(2) That such minor is taught at home in the branches prescribed by law for the same length of time as children are required by law to be taught in the district schools; provided, that a minor legally excused to enter employment may be excused from attending a part-time school or class for the reason that such minor is taught at home the required number of hours.

(3) That such minor is in such physical or mental condition (which must be certified by a competent physician if required by the board) as to render such attendance inexpedient and impracticable.

(4) That no such school is established, or class is taught for the requisite length of time, within two and one-half miles of the residence or the place of employment of the minor, unless free transportation is provided.

(5) That proper influences and adequate opportunities for education are provided for in connection with the employment of such minor.

The evidence of the existence of any such reason for non-attendance must be in each case sufficient to satisfy the superintendent of the district in which the child resides, and the superintendent upon the presentation of such evidence shall issue a certificate stating that the holder is exempt from attendance during the time therein specified.[10]

Any parent, guardian or other person having control of any minor coming within the foregoing provisions who willfully fails to comply with their requirements is guilty of a misdemeanor.[11]

It shall be the duty of the board of education of each district to inquire into all cases of misdemeanor herein defined, and to report the same and the offenders concerned to the juvenile court of the district wherein the offense has been committed; and it is hereby made the duty of the officers of such juvenile court to proceed immediately to investigate and take appropriate action.[12]

All children in any school district between eight and eighteen years of age who in defiance of earnest and persistent efforts on the part of their parents or teachers are habitual truants from school, or while in attendance at school are visious, immoral or ungovernable in conduct, shall be deemed incorrigible, and it is the duty of the board of edu-

---

10. School Laws of the State of Utah, 1951. 75-25-1, pp. 72 and 73.
11. **Ibid.,** 75-25-3, p. 73.
12. **Ibid.,** 75-25-4, p. 73.

cation of each school district to inquire into all
such cases and report them to the juvenile court
for such district, whose duty it shall be to prosecute
such cases as incorrigibles.[13]

Any person over eighteen years of age, who by any
act, words or conduct, or by the omission to do
something required by law to be done, induces any
juvenile to do or to perform any act or to follow
any course of conduct or to deport himself in any
manner that would cause or manifestly tend to
cause such juvenile to become or remain delinquent, or who does any act tending to cause a child
to become or remain delinquent, or who aids, abets,
encourages, contributes to, or becomes responsible
for, the dependency, neglect or delinquency of any
juvenile is guilty of a misdemeanor, and the juvenile court of the county wherein such offense is
committed shall have jurisdiction to administer
such penalty or punishment as is or may be prescribed by law for misdemeanors.[14]

In the foregoing, whenever reference is made to the
board of education, the board, of course operates through
its superintendent of schools and staff. With the approval
of the board of education, the superintendent very commonly delegates authority and responsibility to principals
and coordinators or other assistants.

It will be noted that the parent or guardian, as well
as the child himself, is responsible for the child being in
school. Work permits to enter employment, which the
law sanctions under certain circumstances, are issued by
and at the discretion of the superintendent or his delegated
assistants, and no employer is permitted under this law
and other statutes pertaining to child labor to employ a
minor of school age (under 18) during school hours without being provided with such a legally issued work permit.

---

13. **Ibid.**, 75-26-1, p. 74.
14. **Ibid.**, 14-7-50, p. 100.

The school law has been interpreted by the attorney general to require attendance from the beginning of the regular school year until the law has been fulfilled, rather than permitting the minor of school age to remain out of school at his own discretion until there are only thirty weeks of the school year remaining.[15]

Corporal Punishment   Corporal punishment is not recommended, but the law contains a proviso to the effect that corporal punishment, if administered, must be by permission from the principal of the school in each individual case.[16]

Health of Teachers and Children   In addition to health instruction which becomes functional in application in and out of school, the control, regulation, and promotion of the health of the school child is so interwoven among home, school and community that this area should necessarily be included in this chapter. The following exerpts from state law are quite self-explanatory and are here included in lieu of longer descriptions, explanations and discussions:

Teachers in District Schools Must Be Physically and Mentally Fit.

No person shall be employed by any board of education as teacher in any school district in this state and receive compensation therefor out of any public funds who is mentally or physically disqualified to perform successfully the duties of a teacher, by reason of tuberculosis or any other chronic or acute disease. Any board of education may require any applicant for employment as a teacher to furnish satisfactory evidence that he or she is mentally and physically qualified for the duties of a teacher.[17]

---

15. Ibid., Opinions of the Attorney General, 130, p. 100.
16. Ibid.
17. Ibid., 75-7-20, p. 14.

Health Education—A Requirement for All Teachers

The state board of education shall determine the professional requirements of supervisors of health education and school nurses. Health education consisting of sanitation and personal and school hygiene shall be required of all teachers in the public schools of the state.[18]

Of Parents and Children of Pre-School Age

The board of education of school districts may adopt such reasonable measures for health education and incur such reasonable expense as may be necessary for the promotion of the physical welfare of children of pre-school age in their respective districts, including the education of parents in matters pertaining to child welfare, but the power herein granted to said boards of education shall only be exercised with the consent of the parents.[19] Every pupil in the school from the *first* to *twelfth* grades inclusive shall have instruction in health, hygiene and physical education as provided in the state course of study.[20]

Physiology and Hygiene to be Taught

It shall be the duty of all boards of education and officers in charge of schools and educational institutions supported in whole or in part by public funds to make provision for systematic and regular instruction in physiology and hygiene, including special reference to the effects of stimulants and narcotics upon the human system.[21]

---

18. **Ibid.,** 75-7-21, p. 14.
19. **Ibid.,** 75-7-22, p. 14.
20. Item No. 10 of Standards for Participation in the State School Equalization Fund. July 1, 1937.
21. School Laws of the State of Utah, 1951. 75-16-4, p. 64.

Sanitation and Prevention of Disease
To Be Taught

There shall be established in the state school of education, and in the public schools beginning with the eighth grade, a course of instruction upon the subject of sanitation and the cause and prevention of disease. It shall be the duty of the state board of education and the state board of health, acting conjointly, to prepare a course of study to carry out the provisions of this section.[22]

Tests of Children's Health—By Teachers

It shall be the duty of every teacher engaged in teaching in the public school, separately and carefully, to test and examine every child under his jurisdiction to ascertain if such child has defective sight or hearing, or diseased teeth, or breathes through its mouth. If such test discloses that any child has such defect, the teacher shall notify, in writing, the parents or guardian of the child of any such defect and explain to such parent or guardian the necessity of medical attention for such child.[23]

State Board of Health to Prescribe Rules

The state board of health shall prescribe rules for making such tests and shall furnish to boards of education rules of instruction, test cards, blanks and useful appliances for the carrying out of the purposes of this chapter.[24]

Times for Making

During the first month of each school year after the opening of school, teachers must make the

22. **Ibid.**, 75-16-5, p. 64.
23. **Ibid.**, 75-23-1, p. 71.
24. **Ibid.**, 75-23-2, p. 71.

tests required by this chapter upon the children then in attendance at school, and thereafter as children enter school during the year such tests must be made immediately upon their entrance.[25]

Physicians May Be Employed

The board of education of any school district may employ regularly licensed physicians to make the tests required by this chapter, and when such tests are made by a physician the teacher shall not be required to make the same.[26]

Boards of Education to Enforce Chapter

It shall be the duty of the boards of education of the several school districts to enforce the provisions of this chapter.[27]

Health in Schools

The local boards of health shall have jurisdiction in all matters pertaining to the preservation of the health of those in attendance upon public and private schools, and it is hereby made the duty of each local board of health:

(1) To exclude from school any person, including teachers, suffering with any contagious or infectious disease, whether acute or chronic, or liable to convey such disease to those in attendance.

(2) To make regular inspections of all school buildings and premises as to their hygienic condition, and to report on forms furnished by the state board of health the result of such inspection to those having charge and control of such schools, with instructions as to the remedying of any condi-

25. Ibid., 75-23-3, p. 71.
26. Ibid., 75-23-4, p. 71.
27. Ibid., 75-23-5, p. 71.

tions whereby the health of those in attendance may be impaired or life endangered. A copy of said report shall at the same time be sent to the state board of health.[28]

Delict of School Authorities

In the event of failure or refusal of those having charge and control of such schools to carry out the instructions so given, the board of health shall cause such faulty conditions to be remedied at the proper cost and expense of those having charge and control of the school.[29]

Compulsory Vaccination Forbidden

It shall be unlawful for any board of health, board of education, or any other public board to compel by resolution, order or proceedings of any kind the vaccination of any person of any age; or to make vaccination a condition precedent to attendance at any public or private school in this state, either as pupil or teacher.[30]

It should not be assumed by the reader from the last quotation that there has been general opposition to vaccination. It was felt that this should be a voluntary matter based on education rather than force. For many years there has been a very extensive immunization program of vaccinations and inoculations with the approval and support of enlightened parents.

Handicapped Children   The reader is also referred to Chapter 62 (H.B. No. 68)—*Education of Handicapped Children*[31] which provides for the education of physically handicapped children between the ages of six and eighteen years, defines procedures, provides

28. **Ibid.**, 35-3-8, p. 102.
29. **Ibid.**, 35-3-9, p. 102.
30. **Ibid.**, 35-3-10, p. 102.
31. Utah Code Annotated 1943.

for reimbursements to school districts by the State Board of Education, supervision by the State Superintendent of Public Instruction, cooperation between school districts, and apportionment of costs between cooperating school districts.

Epidemics   Modern health practices call for keeping the schools open during epidemics rather than closing them. This is true of very serious epidemics as well as only moderately serious ones. It has been found by research and carefully evaluated experience that fewer lives are lost and epidemics are controlled in shorter time if the schools are kept open under a plan in which the parents and the schools are especially alerted to look for symptoms and account for every child every morning and afternoon, than if the schools are closed with no opportunity to check regularly on the children and youth of the community.

Daily morning inspection and continuously alert observation results in immediate isolation and care of those with apparent symptoms. Absences are reported within a few minutes after the opening of school and contacts are made with homes of absentees without delay by the school nurse, the health officer, coordinator, principal or member of a committee of cooperating parents. In this way practically all cases of the disease are known and quarantine provisions can be more easily enforced.

During such periods opportunity should be taken with children and parents to develop especially good health citizenship for the benefit of all.

The writer, among others, received first hand a report by the chairman of the State Board of Health that the closing of schools in several districts during the polio epidemic was an unfortunate mistake.[32] It is always regrettable when parents or others, frightened into a spirit of near hysteria, demand the closing of schools when such

---

32. The late Dr. William M. McKay.

action actually does harm rather than the good intended. School and health officials and P.T.A. organizations would do well to see that the members of the community are well fortified with a knowledge of the facts and recommended practices well in advance of the occurrence of any epidemics of contagious disease.

Adult Education   Education is a never ending process and it is highly important that educational opportunities be provided for adults. Adult education has been featured in this state for many years. In fact, as was pointed out in Chapter II, the first class conducted in what is now Utah was for a group of adults. During recent decades federal and state funds have been available for adult education in the school districts of the state and a large number of adults have been reached by the program. This is a more extensive program than many people realize.

The reader will be interested in excerpts from the adult education law which forms the legal basis for this program: [33]

"The general control and supervision of adult education is hereby vested in the state board of education of the state of Utah, except as hereinafter provided."[34]

Every district school board of education in this state may raise and appropriate funds for adult education, determine fees to be levied, if any, and through its superintendent may hire teachers, establish and maintain classes for adults in English, the fundamental principles of democratic government, citizenship, public affairs, worker's education, forums, arts and crafts, general cultural subjects, adult recreation and such other subjects as the state board of education may determine upon. Said classes shall be subject to the regulations of

---

33. Utah Code Annotated, 1943, Vol. 4, Chapter 30.
34. School Laws of the State of Utah, 1951. 75-30-2, p. 90.

the state board of education; and shall be organized to meet the needs of the adults in this state; and as far as practicable, shall be held at such times and places as are most convenient and accessible to the members of the class.[35]

Duties of the state board of education and the state superintendent of public instruction:

(a) The state board shall make and enforce such rules and regulations as it may deem proper, just and necessary for the organization, conduct, and state supervision of the adult education program;

(b) Upon recommendation of the state superintendent the state board may appoint a full time director, and also such other supervisors and assistants as may be necessary or desirable in the administration of this act, and by regulation prescribe the conditions of their employment, fix their remuneration and define their respective duties and powers. The said director under the direction of the state board of education may act as coordinator of the work of said adult education program with any other program of adult education now carried on, or which may be hereafter carried on by the federal government, state government or any of its political subdivisions, or other public agency, or charitable, or educational institution of this state which may wish to cooperate with the adult education program of this act.

(c) The state board shall determine the qualifications of teachers, and issue teaching certificates for teaching adult classes.

(d) The state board shall determine the basis of apportionment among the several districts entitled thereto the funds alloted by the federal govern-

---

35. **Ibid.**, 75-30-3, p. 90.

ment to this state for the purpose of adult education and the state superintendent of public instruction shall apportion said funds in accordance therewith.[36]

For data regarding the funds and enrollment in adult education classes by districts the reader is referred to the current issue of the Utah School Report.[37]

The health program previously referred to in this chapter has definite implications for adult education as has also the work of the P.T.A. and various other organizations in society which engage adults in learning activities.

The extension divisions of the colleges and universities carry on very extensive programs of adult education of far-reaching importance.

Americanization Schools   Part of the state law pertaining to Americanization schools to meet the needs of immigrants reads as follows: The board of education of any school district may, and upon the direction of the state board of education must, establish and maintain for at least two hundred hours during the school year evening school classes in English, the fundamental principles of the constitution of the United States, American history and such other subjects as bear on Americanization, as a part of the public schools; provided, that no board of education shall be required to maintain a class for fewer pupils than a minimum number to be determined by the state board of education. Such classes shall be organized to meet the needs of the persons subject to the provisions of section 75-28-3, and shall be held at places that are most accessible to the members of the class.

36. **Ibid.**, 75-30-4, p. 90.
37. Published biennially by the State Superintendent of Public Instruction.

The state board of education—shall apportion among the several schools districts entitled thereto the funds appropriated for Americanization schools.

75-28-3. All aliens residing in this state, except those who may be physically or mentally disqualified, between the ages of sixteen and thirty-five years, who do not possess such ability to speak, read, and write the English language as is required for the completion of the fifth grade of the public schools shall attend a public evening school class for at least four hours a week during the entire time an evening school class of the proper grade shall be held in session in the district in which he resides and within two and one-half miles of his place of residence, or until the necessary ability has been acquired. [38, 39]

School Lunch   The school and the home again come into close contact in the operation of the school lunch program regarding which the last couple of decades have witnessed a striking development, and for which both federal and state funds are distributed to school districts for the expense of operation. Some surplus federal equipment and commodities have also been diverted to this program. Nourishing meals are served to the pupils for a very nominal charge.

The program which was given great impetus during depression days in the form of W.P.A. projects rapidly developed into a permanent setup to provide warm lunches for all school children whose parents desired to have participate.

There is a full time director and assistants in the State School Office who provide state supervision. Reports

---

38. See School Laws of the State of Utah, 1951, pp. 74-76.
39. Utah Code Annotated, 1943. Vol. 4, pp. 284 and 285.

are filed regularly and are summarized in the biennial reports of the State Superintendent of Public Instruction.[40, 41]

School Policies and the Public   As one thinks of home-school-community relations it becomes apparent that in a democratic society school policies must be understood, accepted, and supported by at least a majority of the citizens. Policies which cannot come to be approved by a substantial majority cannot continue indefinitely and, if not modified, will sooner or later cause dissatisfaction to be registered at the polls at school board elections. The active support and good will of an informed electorate are vital to the continued development and operation of a good program of public education.

BIBLIOGRAPHY

American Association of School Administrators: Twenty-Eighth Yearbook, Public Relations for America's Schools. 1201 Sixteenth Street, N.W., Washington, D. C. 1950.

Cook and Cook: A Sociological Approach to Education. 1950.

Douglass, H. R.: Education for Life Adjustment. New York, Ronald Press, 1950.

Division of Press and Radio Relations, National Education Association: The "PR" Guide, A "Where-to-Look" Handbook of Aids for Your School Public Relations Program. 1201 Sixteenth Street, N.W., Washington, D. C. 1951.

Hand, Harold C.: What People Think About Their

40. Utah School Report. Current Edition. 223 State Capitol, Salt Lake City, Utah.
41. See also School Laws of the State of Utah, 1951, pp. 71 and 72.

Schools. World Book Company, 1948.

Hayes, Wyland J.: The Small Community Looks Ahead. New York, Harcourt, Brace and Company, 1947.

National Citizens Commission for the Public Schools: What Do We Know About Our Schools: 2 West 45th Street, New York 19, N. Y., 1950.

Olsen: School and Community Programs. Prentice Hall, 1949.

N.E.A. Division of Press and Radio Relations: Schools and Fishin' Poles (Also other leaflets and bulletins) 1201 Sixteenth Street, N.W., Washington, D. C.

Provo School Review. Volume I, Number I, and subsequent issues.

Rugg, Harold and B. M. Brooks: The Teacher in School and Society. World Book Co. 1950.

Utah State Department of Public Instruction: School Laws of the State of Utah, 1951.

U. S. Office of Education: World Understanding Begins With Children. Bulletin 1949, No. 17. U. S. Govt. Printing Office, Washington, D. C.

U. S. Office of Education: 102 Motion Pictures on Democracy. Bulletin 1950, No. I. U. S. Govt. Printing Office, Washington, D. C.

U. S. Office of Education: Where Children Live Affects Curriculum. Bulletin 1950, No. 7. U. S. Govt. Printing Office, Washington, D. C.

U. S. Office of Education: Selected Approaches to Adult Education. Bulletin 1950, No. 16. U. S. Govt. Printing Office, Washington, D. C.

U. S. Office of Education: Why Do Boys and Girls Drop Out of School and What Can We Do About It? Circular No. 269. U. S. Govt. Printing Office, Washington, D. C.

CHAPTER XII

PROFESSIONALISM IN EDUCATION AND THE ORGANIZED PROFESSION

Meaning of Professionalism
Education is a profession which should merit the expression of the highest type of professional attitudes and professional performance on the part of its membership. Among the essential and worthwhile experiences of the teacher is participation in the activities and work of professional organizations leading to growth in professionalism. Professionalism involves an attitude of mind, a feeling of respect and pride in belonging to a professional group, an active desire to render service effectively, and the facing of objective reality regarding the needs and problems of the profession in relation to its own membership and to the society which it serves.

There are many important aspects and characteristics of a profession which receive attention in various ways, but there are at least five basic characteristics of a profession without which a field of endeavor could hardly be regarded as a profession. These are:

1. Relatively high standards of entrance and continued growth prescribed for its membership;

2. A body of objective, scientific information, possessed and utilized in large measure by the membership of the profession, and constantly being augmented by further research and the application of professional skills and techniques;

3. Strong service motives which activate the members to render unselfish service in terms of the needs of those who are to be served.

4. Active membership in professional organizations seeking to improve the profession.

5. A code of ethics which guides the actions of the individual members and through which the profession governs itself.

Selective Admission   The necessity for carefully selecting our teachers from among the more capable and well balanced members of society would seem to be clearly self-evident. In addition to general admission to the higher institutions, colleges and schools of education are operating systems of selective admission to programs of teacher education which are designed to lead to employment in the public schools. The reader should be aware of the kind of such program in operation at the professional school of his choice.

In most of these programs at least two important phases of admission are carried on. The one involves the necessity of sifting carefully the candidates for teacher education so as to avoid including in the profession those who show insufficient evidence of probable success in teaching as indicated by a combination of the best available criteria which we have at our disposal. The right kind of guidance should, early in the program, kindly and understandingly direct into other fields those whose personalities, aptitudes, and ways of living make them unfitted for teaching. Sooner or later the decision must squarely be faced as to whether or not it is in the interest of the children in the schools, or even of the candidates themselves, to permit certain of these candidates to try to become teachers. The responsibility for this decision cannot safely be neglected without leaving to the children in the schools the price of such neglect. It must be recognized that teaching in our public schools is not a right to be demanded by any citizen in a democracy; rather, it is a privilege to be granted by society in the interest of those to be taught and in the interest of the common good which may accrue to society by safeguarding the teaching profession.

The other phase of the program recognizes the need

for seeking out the highly desirable young members of
our society of senior high school and college age and encouraging them to prepare for the teaching profession under conditions which clearly justify this encouragement.
It appears that discriminating selective recruitment with
effective person to person follow-up may be helpfully carried on through the organized profession by local, state,
and national teachers associations, by elementary, high
school, and college teachers, and by school administrators
and supervisors who themselves serve in such a way as to
inspire confidence and respect for the profession. For a
keen well-balanced student of excellent personality to be
approached by his highly successful teacher with the sug-
gestion that there is evidence that he too would likely find
success and satisfaction in such service is a compliment of
the highest order.

*Objective,
Scientific
Information*   The body of objective, scientific information characteristic of, produced by, and
available to the membership of the profession of education is not only immense at
the present time, but is expanding continually at such a
rate as to make it a considerable problem to keep in close
touch with even a significant part of it. One must, of
course, be intelligently selective in the process. There will
always be need and ample room for contributions to this
great body of scientific information and for inservice professional growth through discriminating application of
selected materials of the profession. It is not enough that
this body of scientific information should exist and continually increase, but it must be possessed and intelligently
utilized in large measure by the membership of the profession through pre-service and inservice education.

*Service
Motive*   The service motive waxes especially strong
among the devoted teachers of the state and the
nation who show real concern for the optimum
development of the personalities and capacities of each
pupil as a cooperating member of the democratic society.

The real teacher is characterized by genuine friendliness and individual helpfulness based on skilled observation and objective analysis of the needs of each pupil as well as of the group as a whole. He is imbued with faith in the democratic processes and carries great loyalties for real democracy which he attempts to enhance through his work. It would be difficult to find any other group of comparable size made up of people who are more loyal than are the teachers of America.

Membership in Professional Organizations   Professionalism calls for active membership and participation in the official organizations of the profession. While still in the pre-service preparation period, prospective teachers should feel the fellowship of affiliation with student chapters of the National Education Association and state education association, Association for Childhood Education, Phi Delta Kappa, Delta Kappa Gamma, and other comparable organizations.

The very minimum membership obligation that should be expected of any teacher in service is continuous membership in the local association, the state association, and the National Education Association, preferably under a plan of combined membership. Any teacher who neglects membership in any one or more of these three is receiving benefits from the loyalties of others without providing his minimum share of support to the organized profession. Memberships in other very worthy organizations of the profession should be in addition to and not as a substitute for any of the above three which are expected to include the members of the entire profession.

It is recommended that steps be taken effectively to acquaint prospective teachers and those already in service with the organization and programs of the various professional associations, including the following:[1]

National Education Association of the United States

---

1. This is certainly not a complete list and you may wish to add others.

with its sections and affiliated organizations.
The Utah Education Association[2] with its sections
   and affiliated groups
The local teachers association
Various Associations in designated subject and special
   interest areas
Association for Childhood Education International
Phi Delta Kappa
Delta Kappa Gamma and similar organizations
American Council on Education
World Education Fellowship
National Association for the Study of Education
World Organization of the Teaching Profession
United Nations Educational, Scientific, and Cultur-
   al Organization.

Code of
Professional
Ethics
Codes of ethics have evolved through
the years out of the experience of the profession with the help of officials, special
committees, and the support of the mem-
bership. These codes are intended not alone for discussion
purposes, although discussion is important, but as real
guides to professional behavior and performance.

The present code of ethics of the Utah Education Association as a successor to previously recognized codes of
the organization was prepared by the U. E. A. Professional
Relations Committee and recommended to the House of
Delegates on October 11, 1945, for adoption as the official
code of the association. It was published in the December,
1945, issue of the Utah Educational Review to give the
membership an opportunity to study and discuss it carefully before its adoption. It became the official code of the
Utah Education Association on April 20, 1946, by action
of the House of Delegates. This code and also the N. E. A.

2. Also similar associations for other states.

code are here reproduced for purposes of study and discussion as well as a present and future guide toward greater professionalism.

Code of Ethics of the Utah Education Association

1. Teaching is a profession that merits our utmost loyalty and devotion. We will undertake our work whole-heartedly and enthusiastically as a profession worthy of the best efforts of the most capable—a commendable life's work and not a temporary stepping stone.

2. In teaching, as in all worthy professions, growth is essential to life. We will keep abreast of progress and in touch with the advancement of vital interests of the profession and of those whom we serve. We will employ every effective means of growing professionally, such as the reading of books and magazines, active affiliation with local, state, and national education associations and other related organizations, organized study programs, attendance and participation in faculty meetings, discussion groups, institutes, and conventions. We will recognize the importance of being scholastically and professionally prepared for the positions we seek or accept.

3. In any profession service is of paramount importance. As teachers we will always endeavor to render the highest quality of service of which we are capable in terms of the needs of our students and of society, irrespective of the amount of compensation. However, we will not be unmindful of the importance of adequate financial compensation for professional service through the operation of an equitable and adequate salary schedule.

4. We believe in democratic cooperation in a

spirit of courteous helpfulness and sympathetic understanding. We will strive earnestly to teach democracy though living democracy in our personal and professional relations with pupils and patrons, and with fellow teachers, supervisors, and administrators.

5. Ethical teachers are truly patriotic in the deepest and best sense. We believe in humanity and in the ideals of our country as a worthy member of the world family of nations organized to promote peace and progress for all people. As good citizens, we will participate in the activities of the community, and especially in those activities that have to do with the protection and betterment of the immature.

6. We believe in the improvability and educability of persons and peoples, and we affirm our faith in the great power of democratic education as an agency for both individual and social progress.

7. Recognizing that schools exist for the learners, we will be mindful of the influence of the teacher's personality on the developing personalities of children and youth. We believe that the teacher who is a pessimist, a grouch, or a cynic has no legitimate place in the school room.

8. Ethical teachers are dependable. We will respect the terms and the spirit of every appointment and contract into which we enter and expect others to do likewise. We will neither claim nor assume any special cancellation privilege which we would be unwilling to have exercised by the board of education under the terms of the contract.

9. We will be loyal to other members of the profession and strive to enhance their influence for good among pupils, fellow teachers, and mem-

bers of the community. We will avoid unfavorable criticism of associates except when professionally made to proper officials, and then only on the basis of verifiable facts and conditions. We will, however, feel professionally obligated to report unethical and harmful practices to the proper officials as a helpful means of safeguarding the important services of the school.

10. We believe that teacher placement in the public schools is a public service in the public interest, chargeable to public funds, and we deem it professionally unethical for teachers to be charged or made to pay private commissions for being placed in positions.

11. We believe that admission to programs of specific preparation for teaching, which may lead to employment in the public schools, is a privilege to be granted by society on the basis of merit and aptitude and is not a right to be demanded and claimed by any citizen. We will, therefore, encourage the more capable and desirable young people (as judged by a combination of the best available criteria) to enter the field of preparation for teaching on the basis of sound programs of selective admission.

12. Although recognizing the desirability or having the position seek the person, when applying for a position we will make application to the properly designated official. We will not apply for a specific position that is not vacant, nor will we underbid others or underbid the salary schedule in an effort to obtain a position. After signing a contract we will not make further applications to other districts except for the period following the legal expiration of the contract. We will likewise expect employing officials of other districts to clear with our superintendent of schools before

offering us a contract which entails the cancelling of the one we have already signed.

13. We will not solicit or accept private fees for educational work which interferes with or is cov· ered by the contracts for service which we have signed with the school or school district, and we will not unethically require of pupils private lesson work from ourselves as a prerequisite to admission to courses or classes in the school.

14. Testimonials regarding teachers should be truthful, unevasive, and confidential, and should be sent directly to the prospective employer or institution desiring information about the teacher. We will, therefore, neither issue nor seek "to whom it may concern" recommendations which are carried in hand.

15. As professional teachers we will avoid the endorsing of educational materials for mere personal gain or for any other reason except upon the basis of the honest merits of the educational books or other materials which we conscientiously and ethically desire to recommend to teachers or to the public.

16. Although as teachers we claim all honorable rights as citizens of our democracy, including the right of protection from the damaging influence of petty prejudices, yet we recognize that the nature of the educative process which we direct requires that the conduct of the teachers conform to the desirable patterns or standards of behavior of the better and more wholesome members of the community.

17. We will have reverence for all that is good, and so teach that we will encourage in our pupils the development of the fundamental virtues involved in the good life. We will respect as sacred

the right of each individual to his own religious faith and worship, and we will neither seek to impose upon those we teach our own religious creed nor express antagonism to theirs.

The National Education Association
Code of Ethics

Preamble—Believing that true democracy can best be achieved by a process of free public education made available to all the children of all the people; that the teachers in the United States have a large and inescapable responsibility in fashioning the ideals of children and youth; that such responsibility requires the services of men and women of high ideals, broad education, and profound human understanding; and, in order that the aims of democratic education may be realized more fully, that the welfare of the teaching profession may be promoted; and, that teachers may observe proper standards of conduct in their professional relations, the National Education Association of the United States proposes this code of ethics for its members. The term "teacher" as used in this code shall include all persons directly engaged in educational work, whether in a teaching, an administrative, or a supervisory capacity.

Article I—Relations to Pupils and the Home

Section 1—It is the duty of the teacher to be just, courteous, and professional in all his relations with pupils. He should consider their individual differences, needs, interests, temperaments, aptitudes, and environments.

Section 2—He should refrain from tutoring pupils of his classes for pay, and from referring such pupils to any member of his immediate family for tutoring.

Section 3—The professional relations of a teacher with his pupils demand the same scrupulous care that is required in the confidential relations of one teacher with another. A teacher, therefore, should not disclose any information obtained confidentially from his pupils, unless it is for the best interest of the child and the public.

Section 4—A teacher should seek to establish friendly and intelligent cooperation between home and school, ever keeping in mind the dignity of his profession and the welfare of the pupils. He should do or say nothing that would undermine the confidence and respect of his pupils for their parents. He should inform the pupils and parents regarding the importance, purposes, accomplishments, and needs of the schools.

Article II—Relations to Civic Affairs

Section 1—It is the obligation of every teacher to inculcate in his pupils an appreciation of the principles of democracy. He should direct full and free discussion of appropriate controversial issues with the expectation that comparisons, contrasts, and interpretations will lead to an understanding, appreciation, acceptance, and practice of the principles of democracy. A teacher should refrain from using his classroom privileges and prestige to promote partisan politics, sectarian religious views, or selfish propaganda of any kind.

Section 2—A teacher should recognize and perform all the duties of citizenship. He should subordinate his personal desires to the best interests of public good. He should be loyal to the school system, the state, and the nation, but should exercise his right to give constructive criticisms.

Section 3—A teacher's life should show that education makes people better citizens and better neighbors. His personal conduct should not needlessly offend the accepted pattern of behavior of the community in which he serves.

Article III—Relations to the Profession

Section 1—Each member of the teaching profession should dignify his calling on all occasions and should uphold the importance of his services to society. On the other hand, he should not indulge in personal exploitation.

Section 2—A teacher should encourage able and sincere individuals to enter the teaching profession and discourage those who plan to use this profession merely as a stepping stone to some other vocation.

Section 3—It is the duty of the teacher to maintain his own efficiency by study, by travel, and by other means which keep him abreast of the trends in education and the world in which he lives.

Section 4—Every teacher should have membership in his local, state, and national professional organizations, and should participate actively and unselfishly in them. Professional growth and personality development are the natural product of such professional activity. Teachers should avoid the promotion of organization rivalry and divisive competition which weaken the cause of education.

Section 5—While not limiting their services by reason of small salary, teachers should insist upon a salary scale commensurate with the social demands laid upon them by society. They should not knowingly underbid a rival or agree to accept a salary lower than that provided by a recognized schedule. They should not apply for positions for the sole purpose of forcing an increase in salary in their present positions; correspondingly, school officials should not refuse to give deserved salary increases to efficient employees until offers from other school authorities have forced them so to do.

Section 6—A teacher should not apply for a specific position currently held by another teacher. Unless the rules of a school system otherwise prescribe, he should file his application with the chief executive officer.

Section 7—Since qualification should be the sole determining factor in appointment and promotion, the use of pressure on school officials to secure a position or to obtain other favors is unethical.

Section 8—Testimonials regarding teachers should be truthful and confidential, and should be treated as confidential information by school authorities receiving them.

Section 9—A contract, once signed, should be faithfully adhered to until it is dissolved by mutual consent. Ample notification should be given both by school officials and teachers in case a change in position is to be made.

Section 10—Democratic procedures should be practiced by members of the teaching profession. Cooperation should be predicated upon the recognition of the worth and the dignity of individual personality. All teachers should observe the professional courtesy of transacting official business with the properly designated authority.

Section 11—School officials should encourage and nurture the professional growth of all teachers by promotion or by other appropriate methods of recognition. School officials who fail to recommend a worthy teacher for a better position outside their school system because they do not desire to lose his services are acting unethically.

Section 12—A teacher should avoid unfavorable criticism of other teachers except that formally presented to a school official for the welfare of the school. It is unethical to fail to report to the duly constituted authority any matters which are detrimental to the welfare of the school.

Section 13—Except when called upon for counsel or other assistance, a teacher should not interfere in any matter between another teacher and a pupil.

Section 14—A teacher should not act as an agent, or accept a commission, royalty, or other compensation, for endorsing books or other school materials in the selection or purchase of which he can exert influence, or concerning which he can exercise the right of decision; nor should he accept a commission or other compensation for helping another teacher to secure a position.

Article IV—Standing Committee
On Professional Ethics

There is hereby established a Standing Committee on Professional Ethics consisting of five members appointed by the president.

It shall be the duty of the Committee to study and to take appropriate action on such cases of violation of this Code as may be referred to it. The Committee shall be responsible also for publicizing the Code, promoting its use in institutions for the preparation of teachers, and recommending needed modifications.

If, when a case is reported, it is found to come from a state which has an Ethics Committee, such case shall immediately be referred to said state committee for investigation and action. In the case of a violation reported from a state which has neither a code nor an ethics committee, or from a state which has a code but not an ethics committee, the NEA Ethics Committee shall take such action as seems wise and reasonable and will impress members with the importance of respect for proper professional conduct. Such action shall be reported to the chief school officers of the community and the state from which the violation is reported. The Committee is further vested with authority to hold hearings and to recommend to the Executive Committee the expulsion of a member of the National Education Association for flagrant violation of this code.

Conclusion   If, as is probably the case, the reader is planning to become a teacher, it is to be seriously hoped that he will be a very helpful, highly successful teacher and a thoroughly professional teacher. Such being the case, there are deep satisfactions awaiting, the like of which are seldom if ever experienced by the teacher of poor or mediocre performance or the teacher with little concern regarding professionalism.

As this chapter and this volume come to a close it should again be recognized that, just as education's service to the individual and to society is a never ending process, so also is teacher education a continuous, never ending process, made up of all the educative experience, formal and informal, of the teacher from the time he first makes the decision to become a teacher until he withdraws from the profession. Pre-service education includes the teacher's preparation preceding the beginning of his first position in the schools and the hope is here expressed that this preparation is being pursued in the right professional manner.

It should, of course, be recognized that with this preparation at its best, the beginning teacher is far from a finished product, but it is hoped that under wise supervision he is ready to make an intelligent and enthusiastic beginning and that he will recognize the need for continued in-service preparation and growth. In-service teacher education includes all of the teachers' educative experience, formal and informal, which follows the period of pre-service preparation. In effectively pursuing this life-giving, continuous growth, it is hoped that the reader will experience first hand the full meaning of Dr. Entorf's statement that "the best of good teaching is associated with the overflow of satisfying life."

BIBLIOGRAPHY

Anderson, Harold A.: "The Preparation of College Teachers" N.E.A. Journal, May, 1951, p. 343.

Barzun, Jacques: Teacher in America. Boston, Little, Brown and Co. 1945.

Law, Reuben D.: Content and Criteria Relating to Professional Teacher Education. University of Southern California, Los Angeles, Calif. 1941.

National Commission on Teacher Education and Professional Standards, N.E.A.: The Education of Teachers as Viewed by the Profession; Report of the Bowling Green, Ohio, Conference. 1201 Sixteenth Street, N.W., Washington, D. C. 1948.

National Commission on Teacher Education and Professional Standards, N.E.A.: The Teaching Profession Grows in Service: Report of the New Hampshire Conference. 1201 Sixteenth Street, N.W., Washington, D. C. 1949.

Utah Education Association: Code of Ethics of the Utah Education Association, Salt Lake City, Utah, 1946.

Moffitt, J. C.: The History of Public Education in Utah, 1946. Chapter XV.

Morgan, Joy Elmer: Our Profession Glorious. Personal Growth Leaflet Number 161. National Education Association. 1201 Sixteenth Street, N.W., Washington, D. C.

National Education Association: Ethics for Teachers. The N.E.A. Code. Personal Growth Leaflet Number 135. 1201 Sixteenth Street, N.W., Washington, D. C.

Woellner and Wood: Requirements for Certification of Teachers, Counselors, and Administrators. Sixteenth Edition, University of Chicago Press. 1951-52.

APPENDIX

I. Scriptural Reference to Education

A. Bible

Proverbs 1:1-5
Proberbs 1:7
Proverbs 1:22
Proverbs 1:28 & 29
Proverbs 2:2 & 3
Proverbs 2:6
Proverbs 2:10 & 11
Proverbs 3:3 & 4
Proverbs 3:13-15
Proverbs 3:19-21
Proverbs 3:35
Proverbs 4:1
Proverbs 4:5-9
Proverbs 4:13
Proverbs 5:1
Proverbs 7:4
Proverbs 8:5
Proverbs 8:10, 11, 12, & 14
Proverbs 9:6
Proverbs 9:9 & 10
Proverbs 10:1
Proverbs 10:11
Proverbs 10:13 & 14
Proverbs 10:21
Proverbs 10:23
Proverbs 10:31
Proverbs 11:9
Proverbs 11:12
Proverbs 12:1
Proverbs 12:8
Proverbs 12:11
Proverbs 12:18 & 19
Proverbs 12:23
Proverbs 13:1
Proverbs 13:10
Proverbs 13:15
Proverbs 13:18
Proverbs 13:20

Proverbs 14:6
Proverbs 14:18
Proverbs 15:33
Proverbs 14:33
Proverbs 15:2
Proverbs 15:7
Proverbs 15:14
Proverbs 16:16
Proverbs 16:21-23
Proverbs 17:24
Proverbs 17:27
Proverbs 18:4
Proverbs 18:15
Proverbs 19:2
Proverbs 19:8
Proverbs 19:20
Proverbs 20:5
Proverbs 20:15
Proverbs 21:11
Proverbs 21:30
Proverbs 22:6
Proverbs 23:12
Proverbs 22:17 & 18
Proverbs 23:12
Proverbs 23:23
Proverbs 24:13 & 14
Proverbs 29:3
Proverbs 29:18
Ecclesiastes 2:13
Ecclesiastes 2:26
Ecclesiastes 7:12
Ecclesiastes 7:19
Ecclesiastes 8:1
Ecclesiastes 9:17 & 18
Ecclesiastes 10:10
Ecclesiastes 10:12
Ecclesiastes 12:12
Matthew 7:7

B. Doctrine and Covenants

D. & C. 6:7 and 11:7

38:23
38:30
42:14
42:57 & 58
47:17 & 18
50:23 & 24
55:4
57:11, 12, & 13
68:25 & 28
72:20
77:4
82:3
84:45
84:85
88:40
88:66 & 67
88:77, 78, 79
88:118
88:119, 122, and 123
88:127, 128, 130, 136
   & 137
88:7 & 13
88:15
93:24
93:26-31
93:36
93:40
93:53
95:10
95:17
97:1
97:3-6
109:6, 7, 8, & 14
121:33
121:42
128:22
130:18 & 19
131:6
136:32

C. Book of Mormon

2 Nephi 2:25
2 Nephi 5:15
2 Nephi 6:26
2 Nephi 9:28
2 Nephi 9:29
2 Nephi 9:39
2 Nephi 9:42 & 43
2 Nephi 9:48
2 Nephi 27:26
2 Nephi 28:15
2 Nephi 28:30
2 Nephi 32:7
2 Nephi 33:6
Mosiah 1:2 & 3
Mosiah 1:4
Mosiah 1:8
Mosiah 2:4
Mosiah 2:17
Mosiah 4:14 & 15
Mosiah 12:27
Mosiah 23:14
Mosiah 24:4
Helaman 5:13
3 Nephi 6:12
3 Nephi 14:7 & 20
3 Nephi 22:13
3 Nephi 23:1
3 Nephi 26:19
3 Nephi 27:29
Mormon 1:2
Moroni 10:9 & 10

D. Pearl of Great Price

Moses 6:6
Moses 6:58
Abraham 1:2
Abraham 1:26
Abraham 3:19
Thirteenth Article of Faith
p. 58.

II. Miscellaneous Quotations

Education is the power to think clearly, the power to act well in the world's work, and the power to appreciate life.

Brigham Young

As man is God once was, and as God is man may become.

Lorenzo Snow

Through the influence of the holy spirit the powers of the human mind may be quickened and increased.

*James E. Talmage*s
Articles of Faith

No faith is worth the keeping unless it be an intelligent faith.

John A. Widtsoe

Knowledge without wisdom gives a troubled life.
Anonymous

We become like the things we do.
Anonymous

We achieve freedom by knowing and living the truth.
Anonymous

The letter killeth and the spirit giveth life.

A little learning is a dangerous thing.
Anonymous

Following the line of least resistence makes rivers and men crooked.

Leo J. Muir

The meaning of life and its measure are to found in the range of things to which we are alive and the degree of that aliveness.

Guy C. Wilson

INDEX

Absentee ballots, 93

Academies established by L.D.S. Church, 47

Academy and College of St. Mary of the Wasatch, 50, 77

Accreditation, 29, 30

Achievements, educationally, 52, 53, 54, 55, 56, 57, 58-64, 70

Active process of learning, 13

Administration, function of, 112

Administrative relationships, 113, 147, 164

Administrative relationships, clearly defined, 15

Admission, selective, 16

Adult education, 27, 34, 70, 80, 199

Agricultural experiment stations, 170

Air University, 168

Air War College, 168

Alaska, natives of, 172

Alcohol and narcotics, 74, 109

All Hallows College, 50

Allen, Hollis P., 61, 172, 177, 178

Americanization schools, 77, 201

American Association of Colleges for Teacher Education, 30

American Association of School Administrators, 19, 30, 39, 164, 178, 203

American Association of School Administrators, Platform, 194 Resolutions, 22ff.

American Council on Education, 209

American Education, purpose of, 21

American Indians, 172

Anderson, Harold A., 220

Annapolis Naval Academy, 168

Annual reports, 99, 100, 101

Appendix, 222ff.

Appropriations, Federal for education, 166

Approval of building plans and specifications, 143

Arm of state, school district is, 16-17, 67, 68, 90, 92

A.R.O.T.C., 168

Assistant state superintendents, 67, 84

Association for Childhood Education International, 208, 209

Attendance compulsory, 17, 32

Attendance data, 78

Audio-visual, 20, 30, 21, 32

Audit, 102, 141

Authority, joint rather than individual, 97

Authority of expertness, 15

Authority with responsibility, 15

Avenues to the Public, 184

Average years of schooling completed by adult population, 54, 55, 56, 57, 70

Background influences, 41

Balance sheet of the states, 59

Balanced growing, 13, 75, 115, 122

Bancroft, 78

Barnett, Owen L., 3

Barr, A. S., 16

Barzun, Jacques, 220

Bateman, E. Allen, 3, 18, 40, 111, 145, 151

Beecher, Henry Ward, 120

Benjamin, Harold, 80, 150

Bennion, M. Lynn, 44, 47, 63

Bennion, Milton, 73, 78

Bibliographies, 39, 40, 63, 64, 78, 79, 89, 110, 128, 144, 145, 150, 151, 160, 161, 178

Big Horn Academy, 47

Bird Day, 109

Blind and deaf, schools for, 77, 80, 173

Boards of education, local, 15, 22, 25, 36, 37, 67, 68, 69, 92-98, 140, 196
    Election, term of office, 93, 94
    Compensation and expense, 95

Board of education, state, 15, 19, 29, 36, 66, 67, 80, 89, 200, 202
    Election, term of office, 81
    Compensation and expense, 85

Board of Health, local, 195, 196

Board of Health, state, 78, 195

Board of Regents, 147

Board of Trustees, 147

Body Corporate, 96

Bond, 100

Bonded indebtedness, 142

Branch Utah State Agricultural College, 77, 150

Brigham Young College, Logan, 48

Brigham Young University, 47, 48, 49, 77, 150

Brooks, B. M., 204

Bryan, William Cullen, 120

Buck, Paul H., 57

Budget officer, 98, 99, 139,

Budgets, 37, 87, 98, 129, 139, 140, 148

Building reserve fund, 141

Buildings, 24, 28, 86, 141, 143

Burton, William H., 39

Butts, R. F., 64

Byron, Lord, 120

Campbell, Roald F., 111

Canal Zone, 171

Cannon, Tracy Y., 48

Capital outlay, 141, 142

Carbon College, 77, 150

Cassie Stake Academy, 47

Caswell, Hollis L., 123, 126

Cathedral, School, 50

Catholic schools, 50, 77

Cattell, 58

Census, 41, 54, 101, 134

Central Utah Vocational School, 76

Certification of teachers, 35, 36, 80, 87, 99, 100, 103, 149

Chamberlain, 39

Chamber of Commerce Committee on Education, 18, 40, 43, 56, 64, 145

Character education, 14, 21, 26, 73, 74, 75, 109, 175, 213, 214

Charts, 8

Chase, Francis L., 61, 62, 131

Chief state school officer, 29, 66, 67, 76, 84, 141, 201

Child, 31

Child labor, 32

Children of U. S. officials and employees abroad, 171

Childs, J. S., 64

Choices, in relation to democracy, 14

Church and state, separation of, 27, 45, 46, 66, 73, 76

Church organization as an influence, 52, 53

Citizenship, 26, 31, 32, 34, 35, 73, 215

City School districts, 68, 69, 92

Civic mindedness, 50
Clark, Ervin, 125, 126
Classroom unit, 135
Class size, 36
Clerk of board, 95, 100
Clive, Baron Robert, 120
Coast Guard Academies, 168
Code of Ethics, 16, 33, 206, 207ff.,
214ff.
Colleges and schools of education,
87
College and university of educa-
tion, 46, 47, 49, 76, 77, 146ff.,
166, 173, 175, 176
Combined membership, 208
Command and General Staff
School, 168
Committee of the whole, 96
Committee, serving on, 15
Communists, 27
Community Coordinating Coun-
cils, 75, 188
Community life, 45, 71, 180
Community school, 180
Compulsory attendance, 17, 32,
189
Compulsory retirement, 157
Conduct of teachers, 33, 200, 213
Conservation of human and nat-
ural resourses, 20, 26
Consolidation 17, 19, 22, 29, 48,
52, 53, 68, 69, 70, 71, 72, 73,
91, 92, 106
Constitution, 65, 66, 75, 80, 109,
149, 162
Constitutional amendments, 132,
133
Constitutional oath of office, 94
Constitutional rights, 33
Constitutions and education, 16,
17, 66, 75, 80
Continuous growth and planning,

16, 53, 210, 216
Contracts, 211, 212, 213, 217
Controversial issues, 14, 32, 33,
215
Cook, 203
Cooperation, cooperative plan-
ning, 14, 22, 29, 30, 31, 39,
210
Cooperation with American Re-
publics Program, 171, 172
Cooperative Study of Secondary
School Standards, Evaluative
criteria, 127
Corporal punishment, 193
Coulter, Kenneth C., 125, 127
Council of State Governments,
12, 14, 19, 39, 61, 62, 64, 72,
78, 89, 111, 129, 131, 143, 144,
151, 173, 178
Counties, 68
Courses of study, 108, 149
Course of study committee, 80,
87
Cowdery, Oliver, 44
Cowles, Le Roy E., 49, 71, 78
Criticism, constructive, 14, 212,
215, 218
Curie, Madam, 120
Curricula, 31, 73, 109, 149

Darwin, Charles, 120
Davies, Daniel R., 111
Deaf and blind, schools for, 77,
80
Delta Kappa Gamma, 208, 209
Democracy, education essential to
12, 211
Democratic organization and pro-
cedure, 13, 15, 210, 211, 217
Denominational schools, 49, 50
Departmentalization, 122, 123
Department of State, 171, 172

Deseret News, 50, 54, 55, 78

Dewey, John, 12

Dilworth, Mary Jane, 45

Directory, State School, 79, 84, 151

Disability retirement, 157

Discipline, 114, 115, 116, 117, 118, 119, 127

Display of flag, 104

District owned busses, 107

District School Fund, 133, 135

District, size of, 17, 19, 22, 29, 36, 129

Districts, number of in each of forty-eight states, 72

Dixie College, 47, 49, 77, 150

Dixon, H. A., 151

Douglas, H. R., 127, 203

Early school district organization, 71

Early schools, 44, 45, 46, 47

Early territorial and state aid, 134

Early, William A., 187

Eastern Arizona Junior College, 47, 49

Education, an investment in progress, 18

Education, a state function, 16, 17, 35, 65

Education, definition of, 11, 12

Education, essential to democracy, 12

Educational Achievements, 52, 53, 54, 55, 56, 57, 58, 59-64

Educational dividends, 18

Educational Policies Commission, NEA, 14, 26, 39, 78

Educational Television, 184

Efficiency of schools, 54, 55, 56, 57, 58, 59-64, 70

Effort, 130

Election, special, 142, 143

Eliot, George, 120

Emery Academy, 47

Employees, appointment of, 113

Enrollments and school population, 24, 27, 49, 50, 57, 58, 78, 148

Enrollments in colleges and universities, percentage of population, 57, 58, 70, 76

Enrollments in 109 nations, 60, 61

Entering and leaving building, 114, 115

Entorf, 16, 220

Environments, socially desirable, 31, 32, 75

Epidemics, 198

Equalization of Educational Opportunity, 18, 29, 37

Equalization Fund, 133

Equipment, materials and supplies, 22, 24

Evaluative Criteria, 127

Evans, Mary Ann, 120

Exceptional children, 36, 77

Expelled from school for inability to learn (Table VI), 120

Experiences, satisfying, 14, 32

Extension of home life, 114, 115

Extension services, 170, 201

Facilities, school use of, 22

Facts, provision for gathering and studying, 19

Farley, Belmont, 184

Faunce, 127

Federal aid to education, 22, 23, 28, 32, 35, 37, 46, 65, 76, 77, 146, 162-179, 199

Federal appropriations for edu-

cation, 166
Federal constitution, 65
Federal central opposed, 28, 37
Federal Government and education, 162-179
Federal Security Agency, 162, 169
Federal surplus, 176
Fees, 17, 146, 149
Fielding Academy, Paris, Idaho, 47
Figures, 8
Films, 285 ff.
Financial autonomy of boards of education, 38
Financing education, 19, 27, 28, 29, 31, 34, 37, 38, 46, 55, 62, 76, 78, 80, 86, 94, 100, 106, 129-145, 146, 201
First schools in Utah, 44, 45
Flag, display of, 104
Foshay, 126
Freedoms, 33, 116, 118
Free public education, 17, 21, 23, 27, 35, 36, 37, 38, 66
Fulbright Program, 171
Fuller, Edgar, 178
Fulton, Robert, 120

Garber, Lee O., 111
General federal aid to education issue, 177, 178
Gila Academy and College, 47, 49
Ginsberg, Sadie D., 125, 127
Gladstone, 120
Goethe, 120
Goldsmith, Oliver, 120
Good and the better, 12
Good life, service to, 16
Governing bodies of educational institutions, 146, 147

Governor, 88, 89
Grants-in-aid, 166
Grouping, 124
Growing, balanced, 13, 75
Growth, areas of, 13, 31, 75
Gruenberg, 118
Guidance, 32, 73, 74
Guiding principles, 11

Hancey, J. Everett, 125, 127
Hand, Harold C., 203
Handicapped children, 197
Hansen, George H., 73
Hartvigsen, 185
Harvard Committee comparative study, 57
Hasler, Fred W., 111
Hawkins, 181
Hayes, Wyland J., 204
Health, 32, 35
Health education, 194
Health examinations, 195
Health of pre-school children, 194
Health of teachers and children, 193-199
Henager School of Business, 77
Henry, Patrick, 120
High School enrollments per 10,-000 population, 54, 70
High School Fund, 133
High school graduates per 1000 population, 54, 70
High schools, 48, 49
Historical Society of Utah, 78
Hoggan, Ila, 48
Holidays, 109
Home - school - community relations, 180-205
Hood, Charles E., 125, 127
Housing and Home Finance Agency, 167

Housing of faculty members and students, 173

Hughes, Raymond M., 40, 58, 61, 64, 78, 130

Huxley, 120

Illiteracy, 34

Income, per cent for education, 131

Income tax, 133

Indebtedness, 142

Indian Affairs, Bureau of, 172

Individual and society, 13

Individual child, understanding of, 119

Individual differences, 119, 121, 124

Individual school, organization and management, 112ff.

Individualized teaching, 22

Individual, respect for, 20, 52

Inflation, 24

Initiative, use of, 15, 109

Institutes, 49

Integration, 13, 75, 122

Intermountain Indian School, 77

International educational relations, 171

Investment in progress, 18

Isolated projects, 171

Issues, controversial, 14

Jacobsen, Ernest A., 3

Jefferson, Thomas, 54

Jewell, J. R., 120, 189

Johnson, Samuel, 120

Joint Committee on Educational Television, 184

Joint rather than individual authority, 97

Juarez Academy, 47, 49

Judge Memorial High School

and Elementary School, 50, 77

Junior colleges, state, 77, 80, 147

Junior high, 122

Kelley, 127

Kilpatrick, William H., 40, 118

Kindred, 39

Knight Academy, 47

Koopman, 40

Lancelot, William H., 40, 58, 61, 64, 78, 130

Land grants, 144, 174-177

Lands, school, 144

Lanham Act, 170

Latter-Day-Saints Colleges, 48

Law enforcement, 75

Law, Leda, 3

Law, Reuben D., 1, 16, 40, 74, 123, 127, 189, 220

Laws, School Laws of the State of Utah, 17, etc.

Lay participation, 22, 29

L.D.S. Business College Branch of B.Y.U., 48, 49, 77

L.D.S. McCune School of Music and Art, 48, 49, 77

L.D.S. University, 48

Leaders per unit of population, 58

Learning, kinds of, 13, 31 active process, 13

Lee, Doris, 123, 127

Lee, J. Murray, 123, 127

Leeway, local, 138

Legal basis for school system, 65, 67, 68, 71

Legal holidays, 109

Legal restrictions on board members, 94, 140

Length of school year, 36

Liabilities, 103, 104, 107, 108

Libraries, school and public, 88, 109
Library of Congress, 172
Lillywhite, Ray L., 154, 156, 159
Lindman, 145
Line and staff organization, 105
Linneaus, 120
Liquor consumption, 52
Local initiative, 15, 19, 29
Local leeway, 138
Local teachers association, 208, 209
Logan Academy, Mt. Pleasant, 50, 77
Lowell, James Russell, 120
Loyalties, 16, 215
Lunch, school, 174, 202

Majority, decisions of, 14
Man, an end in himself, 13
Management, school, 115
Map of Utah school districts, 9
Maratime Academies, 168
Marke, David, 111
Maturation, 13
McCune School of Music and Art, 48, 49, 77
McGrath, Earl J., 29, 162, 165, 169, 178
McKay, William M., 198
Medical education, 169
Meil, 40
Men and Women of great ability, 58
Merchant Marine Academies, 168
Merrill, Amos N., 73
Messenger, 121, 127
Michigan plan of land grants, 175
Military Academy, West Point, 168

Military education, 168
Military service, 23
Millard Academy, 47
Miller, William P., 3
Minimum requirements, 138
Minimum School Program, 133, 135
Miscellaneous quotations, 224
Misner, Paul, 40
Mission schools, 49
Moffitt, J. C., 3, 44, 45, 53, 64, 69, 71, 79, 134, 135, 220
Monroe, W. S., 124, 127, 175, 178
Moral and spiritual values, 14, 20, 21, 26, 39, 40, 73, 78, 175, 213
Morgan, Joy Elmer, 220
Mormons, 41
Morphet, Edgar L., 62, 131, 145, 179
Morrill, A. Reed, 3
Morrill Act of 1862, 176
Mort, Paul R., 144
Motion pictures, 30, 32
Murdock Academy, 47

Naegele, Raymond J., 125, 127
Napoleon, 120
Narcotics, 74, 109, 194
National Association for the Study of Education, 209
National board of education recommended, 28, 164
National Citizens Commission for the Public Schools, 183, 204
National Commission for the Defense of Democracy Through Education, 80, 88, 89, 183, 184
National Commission on Teacher Education and Professional Standards, 30, 220

National Education Association, 24, 26, 30, 31, 33, 40, 62, 111, 179, 208, 214, 221

National Education Association Platform, 31

National Industrial War College, 168

National Police Academy, 168

National Science Board, 169

National Science Foundation, 168, 169

National War College, 168

Naturalization, 34, 35

Nauvoo charter, 44

Naval Academy, Annapolis, 168

Neglect of education costly, 18

Newton, Sir Isaac, 120

Nomination of appointees, 98

Notre Dame Elem. and Jr. High, Price, 50

N.R.O.T.C., 168

Oath of office, 100

Objective, scientific data, 207

Occupied areas, 25

Occupied countries, 171

Occupied islands, 171

Ogden Business College, 77

Ohio plan of land grants, 175

Oklahoma plan of land grants, 176

Olsen, 204

Olsen, Marion, 123, 128

One and two teacher schools, 62, 106, 136

Oneida Stake Academy, 47

Ordinances of 1785 and 1787, 175

Oregon plan of land grants, 175

Organization and administration, servant of educative process, 15

Organization, democratic educational, 13, 35, 57, 65ff.

Organization of board, 95

Organizations, professional, 27

Out of state fees, 149

Overview of organization, 65ff.

Ownership of busses, 107

Parent-Teacher Association, 199, 201

Partch, S. E., 57

Partisan controls, free from, 15, 34, 66, 75, 76, 81, 82, 88, 89, 149

Partisan discriminations forbidden, 13, 36, 81, 82, 88, 149

Part-time education, 36

Pasteur, 120

Patriotism, 211

Permanent School Fund, 144, 176

Personality, sacredly important, 13

Pestalozzi, 121

Phelps, William W., 44

Phi Delta Kappa, 145, 208, 209

Philosophy, definition of, 11

Physical examinations, 195

Physical fitness, 32

Physiology and Hygiene, 194

Placement, 32

Placement of teachers, 212

Planning, 14, 16

Population, 41

Positive rather than negative teaching, 117

Pratt, Parley P., 44

President of board of education, 97

President's committee on Education, 17

Presiding officer of board, 70

Press and Radio Relations, N.E. A. Division of, 184, 203, 204

Prevention of disease, 195

Priestly, 120

Principal of school, 70, 99, 102, 112, 113

Principles, 11ff., 129ff.

Private commissions for placement, unethical, 212

Private lesson work, 213

Private schools, 27

Procedure, democratic, 13

Profession, characteristics of, 205

Professional organizations, membership, etc., 27, 33, 34, 62, 208, 216

Professional leadership, 19, 37, 69

Professionalism, 27, 33, 34, 52, 62, 181, 205, 216

Propaganda, 132

Prophets, school of the, 44

Public funds for public schools, 27, 46, 76

Public Health Service, 169

Public hearing, 139, 140, 142

Public relations, 27, 38, 71, 180, 205

Public school system defined, 65, 66

Publicity and Industrial Development, Department of, 143, 145

Pupil and the public, 181

Pupil-Teacher relations, 116ff.

Pupil transportation, 104, 106

Pupils, 102

Purpose of American Education, 21

Purposing, planning, executing, evaluating, 14

Questions about our schools, 183

Racial discriminations opposed, 13, 21

Radio, 32

Rank of Utah educationally, 52-64

Rates of retirement deductions, 154

Ratings by Hughes and Lancelot, 59, 60

Readjusting boundaries of school districts, 91

Records and reports, 125, 126

Recreation, 32, 35, 45

Recruitment of teachers, 21, 26, 207, 216

Relationships, administrative, 113

Religious influence, 41

Remmlein, Madaline Kinter, 40, 111, 160

Reporting to parents, 125

Reports, 85, 86

Requirements, minimum, 138, 139

Research, 167, 168, 169

Responsibility, authority, accompanying, 15

Responsible directly to the people, board, 88, 90

Responsive to the people, 14

Retirement allowance, 157

Retirement as earned income, 160

Retirement board, 152

Retirement compulsory, 157

Retirement, eligibility for, 156

Retirement for disability, 157

Retirement fund, 153

Retirement fund appropriations by state, 155

Retirement, local city systems, 158, 159

Retirement system, benefits to

beneficiary, 158, 160
Retirement system membership required, 156
Withdrawal, 159
Re-entering, 158
Retirement systems, 34, 152ff.
Retirement systems of private institutions, 159, 160
Reusser, Walter C., 144
Ricks College, 47, 48, 49
R.O.T.C., 168
Rowland Hall, 50, 77
Rugg, Harold, 204
Rural education, 36

Safety patrols, 107
Sacred Heart Academy, Ogden, 50
Salaries, 22, 34, 84, 99, 210, 216
Salt Lake Area Vocational School, 76
Salt Lake City Board of Education, 92
Salt Lake Collegiate Institute, 50
Salt Lake Tribune, 57, 58, 79
Salt Lake Stake Academy, 47
San Luis Academy, 47
Sanitation, 195
Satisfying experience, 14
Saucier, W. A., 123, 128
School-Community relations, 27, 38, 71, 73, 74
School district, an arm of the state, 16, 17, 67, 90, 92
School districts, 9, 36, 45, 52, 67, 68, 72
School of the Prophets, 44
School lands, 144
School law, 86
School lunch, 174, 202
School sections of land, 175
Schooling completed by adult

population, 54, 55, 56, 57
Schools, kinds of, 70
Schools responsive to the people, 14
Schools, strength of the nation, 23
Schools, types of, 112
Schrammel and Sonnenbry, 55, 56
Schrammel, H. E., 55
Scientists per unit of population, 58
Scriptural references to education, 41, 42, 43, 222
Scott, Sir Walter, 120
Sears, Jess B., 111
Secondary schools, 121
Secret societies, 124
Secretary of State Board of Education, 84
Sectarian controls and doctrine, freedom from, 15, 31, 34, 66, 75, 76, 82, 88, 149
Selective admission, 16, 27, 206, 212
Selfish interest groups, 18, 181
Seminaries, 49
Servant of educative process, 15
Service motive, 16, 207, 210
Service to the good life, 16
Seward, William H., 119
Sims, Arch, 125, 128
Sites, 141
Size of class, 36
Size of school districts, 19, 22, 36, 129
Smith, George A., 44, 45
Smith, Joseph, 44
Smith-Mundt Act, 171
Snow College Branch of U.S. A.C., 47, 48, 77, 150
Snowflake Academy, 47

Socialism, 18

Society and individual, 13

Some background influences, 41

Some basic, guiding principles, 11

Sonnenbry, E. R., 55

Spears, Harold, 40, 128

Special schools and state agencies, 77

Special tax, 142

Spencer, Herbert, 120

Spiritual and moral values, 14, 20, 21, 26, 39, 40, 73, 78, 175, 213

St. Ann's School, 50, 77

St. John's Academy, 47

St. John's Lutheran School, 50, 77

St. Joseph School, 77

St. Joseph's School, Ogden (Elem. and Jr. High), 50

St. Mary of the Wasatch, Academy and College, 50, 77, 150

Standards, nature of, 119

Standards, professional, 26, 29, 30, 33, 35, 36, 80

State Board of Education, 15, 19, 29, 36, 66, 67, 80

State Board of Health, 78

State Board for Vocational Education, 76, 80

State Council on School-Community Relations, 74

State Department of Public Instruction, 19, 28, 29, 35, 67, 80, 84, 89, 145

State Industrial School, 77

State Historical Society, 78

State School Office Staff, 3, 67, 74, 84

State school systems, six essentials, etc., 19, 28

State Training school, 77

Statehood, admitted to union, 71

Strang, Ruth, 125

Summit Academy, 47

Superintendent of Primary Schools, (1851), 45

Superintendent of Schools, 25, 26, 37, 67, 69, 71, 72, 95, 98, 99, 113, 139

Superintendents, territorial and state, 53, 67, 76, 84, 85, 86, 87, 137, 141, 143, 201

Supervision, 70, 84, 85, 87, 98, 99, 100, 102, 113, 122, 136, 138, 200, 202

Survey of Education in Utah, 79

Swift, Dean, 120

Tables, 8

Tax base, broadening of, 18, 143, 144

Taxation, 37, 38, 71, 133, 136, 137, 140, 142

Teacher, 33, 62, 102

Teacher Education, 16, 26, 29, 30, 33, 36, 39, 62, 75, 149

Teacher-pupil relations, 116ff.

Teacher retirement, 152ff.

Teachers agencies, commercialized, 212

Teaching, 13, 14, 21, 26, 32

Teaching, selective admission to, 16

Television, 30, 31

Television and the FCC, 184

Tenure and advancement, 33, 34, 37

Territorial and state aid, 134

Territories, education in, 171

Test for the teacher, 113, 127

Testimonials, 213, 217

Textbook Commission, 80, 87

Textbooks, 109
Thackeray, 120
Thorndike, Edward L., 58
Tobacco, 109
Transportation, 70
Transportation of pupils, 104, 106
Treasurer of board, 95, 100, 101
Truth, freedom to pursue, 15, 32, 33
Tuition illegal in public elementary and secondary schools, 17 66

Uinta Stake Academy, 47
Unesco, 24, 25, 209
Unexpired term
  State board of education, 85
  District board of education, 94
Uniform School Fund, 133
United Nations, 24
Universal education, 17, 21, 27
University of Deseret, 45, 146
University of Nauvoo, 44, 146
University of Utah, 45, 76, 146, 150
U. S. Chamber of Commerce, Committee on Education, 18, 40, 56, 64
U. S. Commissioner of Education, 49, 87, 162, 164
U. S. Constitution, 162
U. S. Government Printing Office, 166, 179
U. S. Office of Education, 28, 29, 38, 54, 56, 89, 128, 120, 145, 151, 162, 165, 204
Utah Commission for the Blind, 77
Utah Development News, 143
Utah Educational Association, 145, 208, 209, 220
Utah plan of land grants, 175

Utah Public School Directory, 67, 79, 85
Utah State Agricultural College, 76, 77, 150
Utah State Fair Association, 78
Utah State Institute of Fine Arts, 78
Utah school districts (Fig. 1), 9
Utah Schools for Deaf and Blind, 77
Utah School Report, 78, 79
Utah Territory, 45
Utah's educational rank among the states, 52-64

Vaccination and inoculations, 197
Values, system of, 11
Variety of study fields, 150
Veterans Administration comparative report, 57
Veterans education, 57, 167
Vice president of board of education, 97, 98
Vice principal, 112
Vocational education, 36, 76, 80, 166
Vocational rehabilitation, 172, 173
von Humbolt, Alexander, 120
von Liebig, 120
Voting percentages, 50, 51

Wagner, Richard, 120
Wahlquist, John T., 40
War, 39
War congested communities, 28, 37, 170
War surplus commodities and equipment, 173
Wasatch Logan Academy, 50, 77
Wealth, unequal distribution of, 18

Weber College, 47, 49, 77, 150
Webster, Daniel, 120
Welfare, teacher, 34
Welling, 127
West, Franklin L., 3, 47
West Point Military Academy, 168
Westminster College, 50, 77, 150
Westward movement, 52
Wilkinson, Ernest L., 3

Woellner, 221
Wood, 221
Wordsworth, 120
World citizenship, 38
World Education Fellowship, 209
World Organization of the Teaching Profession, 209

Young, Brigham, 44, 45, 48